EXERCISE BOOK

for

Rosa/Eschholz

The Writer's Brief Handbook
Fourth Edition

Prepared by
Christopher A. Bray
Common Ground Communications, Inc.

Longman

New York Boston San Francisco
London Toronto Sydney Tokyo Singapore Madrid
Mexico City Munich Paris Cape Town Hong Kong Montreal

Exercise Book for Rosa/Eschholz, *The Writer's Brief Handbook,* 4th Edition

Copyright ©2002 Pearson Education , Inc.

ISBN: 0-321-09361-5

2 3 4 5 6 7 8 9 10- CRW –04 03 02

A Note to Instructors

Thank you for adopting *The Writer's Brief Handbook* and its companion, *Exercise Book* for *The Writer's Brief Handbook*. This exercise book has been designed to help your students practice the many points made in *The Writer's Brief Handbook*. In general, for each rule in the *Handbook* one or more exercises are presented. Most exercises contain ten problems, and answers for the first five problems are included at the back of this book. A full set of answers is available in a separate publication, entitled the *Answer Key*. Thus, your students can work independently on numbers 1–5 and the remaining problems can be used for homework, quizzes, or as additional practice for students needing help in learning a particular rule or concept.

Format

Each exercise set is explicitly keyed to the rules presented in the *Handbook*; for example, "GRAM 1a" refers you to the section "GRAMmar Essentials," rule 1a. In order to further help you locate material, a table of contents is also provided.

Most of the exercises are double-spaced in order to provide room on the page for students to answer the problem by editing the original—thereby using the same techniques they will need to apply to their own writing.

Instructors who have assigned *The Writer's Brief Handbook* as a textbook may duplicate any or all of these exercises and the answers in the *Answer Key* for distribution to students. The *Exercise Book* may also be purchased by students. In addition, the *Handbook* and the *Exercise Book* are available for purchase as a shrink-wrapped package at a special discount. Instructors interested in additional information on this package discount should call their Allyn & Bacon/Longman representative or toll-free 800–852-3024.

Also available is *The Writer's Brief Handbook Companion Website*, located at www.ablongman.com/Rosa. This site enables instructors to post and make changes to their syllabi; receive the scores of objective tests on grammar, punctuation and mechanics; hold chat sessions with individual students or groups of students; and receive e-mail and essay assignments directly from students.

Table of
CONTENTS

ESL BASIC

SENTENCES

EDITING FOR GRAMMAR

WORD CHOICE

PUNCTUATION

MECHANICS

DESIGN

WRITING AN ARGUMENT / WRITING ABOUT LITERATURE

SPECIAL KINDS OF WRITING

THE RESEARCH PAPER

MLA DOCUMENTATION AND FORMAT

OTHER SYSTEMS OF DOCUMENTATION

SELECTED ANSWERS TO EXERCISES

PREFACE

Good writing demands a lot of hard work from the author: creative thinking, to find a message worth communicating; writing and revising, to express and refine that message; and editing, to polish that message into its most persuasive form for a particular audience. The number and variety of the tasks faced by an author from start to finish can sometimes seem daunting, but writing, like most complex tasks, becomes much more manageable when it is approached as a series of smaller sub-tasks. *The Writer's Brief Handbook* presents writing, revising, and editing as a series of "rules"—the subtasks to be mastered by every author who seeks to produce good work.

Moreover, writing—perhaps more than almost any other "academic" subject—requires active learning. Reading about how to write is just the beginning. You also need to write regularly and consciously apply the rules in *The Writer's Brief Handbook*. This exercise book is designed to help you actively develop your writing skills by providing intensive practice of the points made in the *Handbook*.

The chapters in the *Exercise Book* mirror those in the *Handbook*:

- Chapter 1, Composing (COMP)
- Chapter 2, Paragraphs (PARA)
- Chapter 3, Grammar Essentials (GRAM)
- Chapter 4, ESL Basics (ESL)
- Chapter 5, Sentences (SENT)
- Chapter 6, Editing for Grammar (EDIT)
- Chapter 7, Word Choice (WORD)
- Chapter 8, Punctuation (PUNCT)
- Chapter 9, Mechanics (MECH)
- Chapter 10, Design (DESIGN)
- Chapter 11, Writing an Argument & about Literature (ARGUE/LIT)
- Chapter 12, Special Kinds of Writing (SPECIAL)
- Chapter 13, The Research Paper (RESCH)
- Chapter 14, MLA Documentation and Format (MLA DOCU)
- Chapter 15, Other Systems of Documentation (OTHER DOCU)
- Selected Answers to Exercises

In general, for each rule in the *Handbook* one or more exercises are presented. Most exercises contain ten problems, and answers for the first five are included at the back of this book.

Using This Book

Before beginning an exercise, we suggest you read completely the section in the *Handbook* from which the exercise is drawn. All exercises are cross-referenced to *The Writer's Brief Handbook*; for example, "GRAM 1a" refers you to the section GRAMmar Essentials, rule 1a. If you have trouble with an exercise you can return to the cross-referenced section in the *Handbook*. But be sure to try the exercises first on your own! Once you complete an exercise, you can check your answers to problems 1–5 by referring to the answer section at the back of this book.

Possible Solutions

Many of the exercises present sentences with errors for you to correct. Often there is more than one correct solution. The answer section of this workbook generally only provides you with one possible solution. It is beyond the scope of this workbook to present multiple solutions and discuss the rationale for each. Thus, if your answer for an exercise differs from the one in the answer section and you believe your solution is correct—or you don't understand why the answer given in this book is correct—be sure to see your instructor. English is an impressively flexible language, and you may well have found another equally valid solution.

Typography

In the exercises, type that should be displayed in italics, such as the title of a book, is in *italics*. However, as you will most likely write your answers by hand, you won't have access to italic type. Use, therefore, the comparable editor's mark—underlining—to indicate italics. The answers provided in the book follow this pattern. For example:

Exercise: Whom is the author of *The Hitchhiker's Guide to the Galaxy*?

Correction: Who is the author of <u>The Hitchhiker's Guide to the Galaxy</u>?

Editing versus Rewriting

Your instructor will guide you as to how to use this book, but for many exercises you can make written corrections directly on the page, rather than rewrite the entire sentence to make the needed changes. This is, in fact, how editors mark up manuscripts; so it is not just a shortcut, but good professional technique. It also eliminates the possible introduction of new errors due to miscopying. The answer section, however, presents completely rewritten sentences.

Abbreviations

The following abbreviations are used in the exercises to refer to and label words, phrases, and clauses:

ADJ CLS = adjective (relative) clause

ADV CLS = adverb clause

COORD = coordinating conjunction

CORREL = correlative conjunction

DO = direct object

GER = gerund

INF = infinitive

IO = indirect object

NOUN CLS = noun clause

PA = predicate adjective

PN = predicate noun

PAST PART = past participle

PRES PART = present participle

SUB = subordinating conjunction

Vi = verb, intransitive

Vl = verb, linking

Vt = verb, transitive

Other Resources

Consult the Preface to *The Writer's Brief Handbook* for a complete listing of other resources available to students. Note that a companion website for this book is available at www.ablongman.com/Rosa. This site provides chapter summaries; the course syllabus; Web links keyed to specific sections of the text; and self-scoring tests on grammar, punctuation and mechanics. It also gives students the ability to chat and e-mail classmates and the instructor.

Chapter 1

COMPOSING

COMP 5c, Proofreading

Proofread the writing excerpt that begins on the following page. Mark up the sample essay as you would your own work, making changes on the page. There are twenty-four items that need correction.

For example:

When I travel I always, or at least usually, carry along with me at least teh following items; shave kit, extra socks, and an extra Fifty Dollars folded inside my shoe. These items has bailed me out of more tight situations then I care to mension.

Answer:

indent 5 spaces

When I travel I always, ~~or at least usually,~~ carry along with me at least ~~teh~~ the following items; shave kit, extra socks, and an extra Fifty Dollars folded inside my shoe. These items has bailed me out of more tight situations then I care to mension.

The Perils Of Astroturf

Andy Pellet

As a purist and a sports fan, I am suspicious of changes in my favorite pastimes, namely, baseball and football. In the past too decades, there have been many new developments--some good and some bad. But the most disturbing change is the introduction of artificial turf as a playing surface because it makes the game's unnatural and causes injuries.

This fake grass first appeared on the sporting scene in 1966, according to the Houston Chronicle. The grass in the Houston Astrodome was dying, so in desparation it was replaced by artificial turf. This new surface, manufactured by the Monsanto Company, was appropriately called "AstroTurf". Since the time of its first appearance on the sporting scene in 1966, the living grass in the stadiums and playing fields have been replaced with one form of artificial turf, or another, usually made of green nylon fibers stiched over a cushioned polyester mat, Astro-Turf is still the most common.

What's so great about artificial turf? If real grass was good enough for the sports heros of yesteryear, why shouldn't it be good enough for today's? The proponents of artificial turf have two basic arguments.

The first arguement used a familiar line of reasoning: artificial turf saves money. The field needs less….

Chapter 2

PARAGRAPHS

PARA 1, Unity

Examine each of the following sample paragraphs for unity. First underline the topic sentence of each paragraph. Then cross out any words, phrases, or clauses in the paragraph that do not develop the topic sentence.

For example:

> The most important day I remember in all my life is the one on which my teacher, Anne Mansfield Sullivan, came to me. I am filled with wonder when I consider the immeasurable contrast between the two lives that it connects. It was the third of March, 1887, three months before I was seven years old. The spring had been seasonable and pleasant.

Answer:

> <u>The most important day I remember in all my life is the one on which my teacher, Anne Mansfield Sullivan, came to me.</u> I am filled with wonder when I consider the immeasurable contrast between the two lives that it connects. It was the third of March, 1887, three months before I was seven years old. ~~The spring had been seasonable and pleasant.~~

—modified from Helen Keller, *The Story of My Life*

1. Mental models, our conceptual models of the ways objects work, events take place, or people behave, result from our tendency to form explanations of things. These models are essential in helping us understand our experiences, predict the outcomes of our actions, and handle unexpected occurrences. Unexpected occurrences can happen at any time. We base our models on whatever knowledge we have, real or imaginary, naive or sophisticated.

   —modified from Donald Norman, *The Psychology of Everyday Things*

2. The market is as much a part of your company as you are. After all, it represents one-half of the ledger. To grow, your business must earn the permission of the marketplace. No concept is more important for the start-up entrepreneur. Guarantees are an essen-

tial component. Customers must give your business permission to sell to them. They do this (at least as repeat customers) only after a thorough assessment of you, your product or service, and your operation. This is why Detroit is having trouble selling cars even though they're better built than they were. Fortunately this hasn't been a problem in the U.S. aerospace industry. These cars have to overcome years of bad notices. It will take time to accomplish this. In fact, it may take until there's a complete turnover in the market—until those of us who now think Japanese or German no longer drive.

—modified from Paul Hawken, *Growing a Business*

3. A classical understanding sees the world primarily as underlying form itself. A romantic understanding sees it primarily in terms of immediate appearance. If you were to show an engine or a mechanical drawing or an electronic schematic to a romantic it is unlikely he would see much in it. It has no appeal because the reality he sees is its surface. Dull, complex lists of names, lines and numbers. Nothing interesting. Classification systems may say more about their creators than about the objects being classified. But if you were to show the same blueprint or schematic or give the same description to a classical person, he might look at it and then become fascinated by it because he sees that within the lines and shapes and symbols is a tremendous richness of underlying form.

—modified from Robert Pirsig, *Zen and the Art of Motorcycle Maintenance*

4. At a certain season of our life we are accustomed to consider every spot as the possible site of a house. I have thus surveyed the country on every side within a dozen miles of where I live. In imagination I have bought all the farms in succession, for all were to be bought, and I knew their price. I enjoy walking and find it a healthful relaxation. I walked over each farmer's premises, tasted his wild apples, discoursed on husbandry with him, and took his farm at his price.

—modified from Henry David Thoreau, *Walden*

5. As the rules of chess define the game of chess, linguistic rules define the game of language, which would not exist without them. They are not strict mechanism of cause and effect—one thing simply making another thing happen—but a system essentially open and incomplete, so that it is always capable of novelty. Rules of etiquette close off a system, keeping it uniform and predictable unless the rules are changed. Who is allowed to change these rules? When can such changes be made? Rules of language are indirect and can be used again and again on the same finite set of letters and words, making possible an open universe of new sentences on the closed universe of the dictionary. Dictionaries you will have noticed are printed, not spoken.

   —modified from Jeremy Campbell, *Grammatical Man*

6. Macintosh Way marketing is the *marketing of technology*—finding the right people and getting the right information into their hands. The cost of this approach is not important. Frequently businesses take other strategies which yield different results. The foundation of this approach is that customers have a deep understanding of what they want, how things should work, and what they are willing to tolerate. They are attracted, not intimidated, by innovation and technology. They actually use and like great products.

   —modified from Guy Kawasaki, *The Macintosh Way*

7. The relative strengths of the leading nations in world affairs never remain constant, principally because of the uneven rate of growth among different societies and of the technological and organizational breakthroughs which bring a greater advantage to one society than to another. If, however, too large a proportion of the state's wealth is diverted from wealth creation and allocated instead to military purposes, then that is likely to lead to a weakening of national power over the longer term. Population growth has not shown a demonstrable effect in this pattern of controlled growth.

   —modified from Paul Kennedy, *The Rise and Fall of the Great Powers*

8. The stock market crash of 1929 brought to light substantial inadequacies in financial reporting. Investigations of bankrupt companies showed numerous arithmetic errors and cases of undetected

fraud. The status of healthy companies is largely unknown. The investigations also disclosed the common use of a widely varying set of accounting practices. The 1920s were arguably a time of greater freedom. A principal outcome of these investigations was that the newly formed Securities and Exchange Commission (SEC) required that publicly held companies must annually issue a report to shareholders. The reports are generally distributed via Second or Third Class delivery. The report must contain financial statements prepared by the firm's management and audited by a certified public accountant (CPA).

—modified from Steven Winkler, *The Complete Guide to Finance & Accounting for Nonfinance Managers*

9. Scarcely twenty miles divide Zanzibar from the African mainland, and on a clear day you can plainly see the island from the coast. A motor launch accomplished the journey across the straits in an hour or two and makes a sound frequently reported as terrifying by the local inhabitants. By air the trip is a matter of ten or fifteen minutes. Yet there is an astonishing difference between the island and the mainland shore. In Zanzibar everything is soft and beguiling. The currents in this region are swift. Zanzibar is as relaxing as a Turkish bath.

—modified from Alan Moorehead, *The White Nile*

10. Throughout the inhabited world, in all times and under every circumstance, the myths of man have flourished; and they have been the living inspiration of whatever else may have appeared out of the activities of the human body and mind. It is not appropriate to consider our physical beings as mere biology. It would not be too much to say that myth is the secret opening through which inexhaustible energies of the cosmos pour into human cultural manifestation. Business is not included in this analysis. Religions, philosophies, arts, the social forms of primitive and historic man, prime discoveries in science and technology, the very dreams that blister sleep, boil up from the basic, magic ring of myth. Anthropologists sometimes are the ones to carry out this investigative work.

—modified from Joseph Campbell, *The Hero with a Thousand Faces*

PARA 2b, Development Strategies 1

There are many methods of developing and organizing information both on the scale of the paragraph and the essay as a whole. For example:

Narration: telling a story, most often relating events in chronological order.

Description: describing scenes, most often ordering the items spatially, as a movie camera might capture a scene.

Examples and illustration: citing examples.

Facts, statistics, reasons: using factual information, including numerical summaries.

Definition: providing an extended definition.

Process analysis: explaining a procedure, usually in a step-by-step description.

Comparison and contrast: comparing two things (demonstrating their similarities) and/or contrasting things (demonstrating their dissimilarities).

Analogy: comparing a complex or unfamiliar subject to another topic typically more widely known and understood.

Classification: grouping topics into larger classes on the basis of one or more criteria that demonstrate shared similarities.

Cause and effect: explaining the causal link between two or more subjects.

Mixed strategies: employing more than one of the preceding strategies.

Many of the paragraphs in the preceding exercise use mixed strategies. Referring back to the sample paragraphs on pages 3–6, list for each the development strategy(ies) you think the author uses.

For example: Helen Keller, *The Story of My Life*
Answer: narration
_____

1. Donald Norman, *The Psychology of Everyday Things*:

   _____

2. Paul Hawken, *Growing a Business:*

   _____

3. Robert Pirsig, *Zen and the Art of Motorcycle Maintenance*:

   _____

4. Henry David Thoreau, *Walden:*

   _____

5. Jeremy Campbell, *Grammatical Man:*

_____

6. Guy Kawasaki, *The Macintosh Way:*

_____

7. Paul Kennedy, *The Rise and Fall of the Great Powers:*

_____

8. Steven Winkler, *The Complete Guide to Finance & Accounting for Nonfinance Managers:*

_____

9. Alan Moorehead, *The White Nile:*

_____

10. Joseph Campbell, *The Hero with a Thousand Faces:*

_____

PARA 2b, Development Strategies 2

For each writing assignment listed here, provide one or more development strategies that you could successfully employ to write on that topic. (If necessary, refer back to the list of development strategies on page 7.)

For example: Explain the concept of separation of power within U.S. government.

Answer: definition; illustration

1. Explain how NCAA basketball has changed in the last decade.

2. Discuss the operations of United Nations' peacekeeping forces.

3. Explain the slower-than-expected adoption of recycling.

4. Describe the impact on the US economy of both the budget surplus and the national debt.

5. Describe the most important day in your life.

6. Describe the differences between attending college as an eighteen-year-old compared to returning to school as an adult.

7. Explain what a family is.

8. What is privacy in the electronic age?

9. Discuss homelessness in America.

10. Discuss changes in automobile manufacturing.

PARA 3, Coherence 1

Writers use four principal tools to make their writing coherent: organization, transitions, repetition of key words and phrases, and parallel structures.

After reading the following passage complete the exercises that follow it.

When I was fourteen, my father's last reassignment took my whole family to Kenya for nearly two years. We arrived right after New Year's Day. Our new home, "the station," was twenty-eight miles out into the bush, and every other Saturday my parents, my sister, and I made the long drive into town. The road was rough, a rutted trail in some places, and our Land Rover ground along at never more than thirty miles an hour, all of us sweltering in this mechanical beast. It was an adventure the first few trips, but became a misery after that. On the Saturday just before our first Easter, we were again making the drive, everyone slapping about inside like raggedy dolls, and no one speaking because it was too noisy and because our moods were too close to foul. Suddenly my father yelled "Look," and pointed off to the left side.

He threw in the clutch and we coasted. Everyone in the truck turned to watch. A herd of bok had appeared on the hillside along the road and they were running full tilt. Before I could even finish asking myself why, the reason appeared: a cheetah, running at top speed. Furiously fast but so smooth it seemed to be riding on an invisible rail, the cat cut across the hill, arcing for a trailing bok. And even as I leaned forward to see better, it was already over: down went the cheetah and bok, the cheetah with his jaws wrapped around his prey's throat. Neither animal seemed to struggle. They lay suddenly still together, in a strange embrace. I could hear nothing but the sound of our engine. The two animals did not move, their silent dance of dust and speed and sere grass was done.

"Won't see much of that round here in a few years," said my father, letting the clutch back out too quickly, lurching the Rover. My head bounced hard on the door pillar.

"Ow," I yelled. I pressed my fingers to my right temple, and almost immediately a welt began to rise against my fingertips. The lump felt hot and wet. Was it blood or sweat? Overcoming this distraction, I called out to my father, "Why? I mean, why not?"

"Poaching," said my father without emotion, driving on. I strained in my seat, looking back through the mud-splattered windows, holding my head. The two animals were now out of sight, obscured by the grass. I continued to look back for another several minutes. My family rode on without speaking, the Rover grinding steadily through the landscape.

—Christopher Bray, "Voyages from Home"

1. How is the sample passage organized? (Chronologically? Spatially? Logically?) Explain your choice.

2. Underline the transitional words and phrases in the story. How do they relate to the type of organization used by the author?

PARA 3, Coherence 2

Writers use four principal tools to make their writing coherent: organization, transitions, repetition of key words and phrases, and parallel structures.

After reading the following passage complete the exercises that follow it.

When I worked on a farm, we managed herds. We managed rangeland. Friends managed feedlots. So I am amused but dismayed when someone talks about managing people. You don't ever manage people—you *work with* them. For your business to succeed, you must take exceedingly good care of your people. This is not a chore or a responsibility, it is the most rewarding aspect of being in business, yet it is the area in which most businesses, large and small, fail.

If people are honest about it, you will find that the majority of them are not satisfied with their jobs, their work, or their relationship with "management." One of the strongest reasons so many people want to go into business for themselves is not the allure of business, but a desire to get away from their current stifling jobs. It is well within your power as a businessperson to create an atmosphere that is not stifling.

—Paul Hawken, *Growing a Business*

1. How is the sample passage organized? (Chronologically? Spatially? Logically?) Explain your choice.

2. Underline the words or phrases repeated by the author. What is the effect of this repetition?

PARA 3, Coherence 3

Writers use four principal tools to make their writing coherent: organization, transitions, repetition of key words and phrases, and parallel structures.

After reading the following passage complete the exercises that follow it.

I can see by my watch, without taking my hand from the left grip of the cycle, that it is eight-thirty in the morning. The wind, even at sixty miles an hour, is warm and humid. When it's this hot and muggy at eight-thirty, I'm wondering what it's going to be like in the afternoon.

In the wind are pungent odors from the marshes by the road. We are in an area of the Central Plains filled with thousands of duck hunting sloughs, heading northwest from Minneapolis toward the Dakotas. This highway is an old concrete two-laner that hasn't had much traffic since a four-laner went in parallel to it several years ago. When we pass a marsh the air suddenly becomes cooler. Then, when we are past, it suddenly warms up again.

—Robert Pirsig, *Zen and the Art of Motorcycle Maintenance*

1. How is the sample passage organized? (Chronologically? Spatially? Logically?) Explain your choice.

2. Underline the parallel structures. What is the effect of these structures?

Chapter 3

GRAMMAR ESSENTIALS

GRAM 1a, Verbs

For each of the sentences, underline the verb and related item and label them as follows:

• If the verb is linking, underline both the verb and the predicate adjective(s) or predicate noun(s) (Vl, PA, PN).

• If the verb is transitive, underline both the verb and the indirect or direct object(s) (Vt, IO, DO).

• If the verb is intransitive, underline only the verb (Vi).

For example: Ollie cut the boards.
             Vt   DO

1. Tina swims in the pool on Tuesdays.

2. John gave Fred a birthday present.

3. The weather seems fine today.

4. Shelby bought her textbooks at the campus bookstore.

5. Jorge is a tenor.

6. Bread was delivered to the flood victims by the National Guard.

7. The National Guard gave the flood victims bread.

8. Biotechnology has required a very substantial investment.

9. Nanna wrote me a long letter.

10. Bahna sings for her church choir.

GRAM 1b, Nouns

Complete the following table. Consult a dictionary if necessary.
For example:

SINGULAR	PLURAL	SINGULAR POSSESSIVE	PLURAL POSSESSIVE
pen	pens	pen's	pens'
1. dish			
2. hero			
3. book			
4. wife			
5. man			
6. boss			
7. fish			
8. roof			
9. sky			
10. criterion			

GRAM 1c, Pronouns

Underline the pronouns in the following sentences.
For example: Doris gave <u>it</u> to <u>me</u>, but <u>I</u> told <u>her</u> <u>it</u> wasn't <u>mine</u>.

1. I gave Donald a call.

2. I spoke to him yesterday.

3. He usually has to call me back.

4. Raspberries are ready at their farm.

5. Which farm, McGuire's?

6. Yes, everybody loves their fresh fruit.

7. I often go to the library by myself.

8. Our teacher reminded us to begin our research papers early.

9. Josie's paper on recycling was more interesting than mine.

10. Because the Guggenheim Museum was closed, we went to the Whitney.

GRAM 1d, Adjectives

Choose the correct adjectival form (positive, comparative, or superlative) and underline your selection in each sentence that follows.

For example: Is the Empire State Building still the world's (tall, taller, <u>tallest</u>)?

1. If presented with Häagen-Daz and Ben & Jerry's, could you say which is (creamy, creamier, creamiest)?

2. The *Washington Post* declined to name the (good, better, best) candidate amongst the five potential nominees.

3. Jack is (old, older, oldest) than his brother John.

4. Jack is the (old, older, oldest) of the four children.

5. Before starting the 108 riders, the judge called, "May the (good, better, best) cyclist win!"

6. I've eaten a lot of good strawberry shortcakes, but I still think my mom's is (good, better, best).

7. Khalil and Sollie can never agree which is (fun, more fun, the most fun)—Manhattan Beach or Rockaway Beach.

8. The meteorologist said that yesterday may have been hot, but today would be (hot, hotter, hottest).

9. He also said that last Thursday was the (hot, hotter, hottest) day this summer.

10. Cora told me that the Everglades were (big, bigger, biggest) than Okefenokee Swamp and Great Dismal Swamp.

GRAM 1e, Adverbs

Underline the adverbs in the following sentences.

For example: Things cook <u>more</u> <u>slowly</u> in Denver than Dallas because of the altitude.

1. John runs fast.

2. Of all the sopranos, Lena sang the most beautifully.

3. The commute home always seemed longer than the one to the office.

4. After the thunderstorm, steam rose eerily from the still warm pavement.

5. Jackson was tired but worked hard to finish the assigned reading before going to bed.

6. For a work so famous, Lincoln's "Gettysburg Address" is surprisingly short.

7. High-speed rail may change how frequently we fly to Los Angeles.

8. Ellen was very happy to discover that the most important book in her bibliography had not been checked out of the library.

9. The children of immigrants rarely know much about their parents' homeland.

10. The vase of freshly cut peonies gave the room a wonderful smell.

GRAM 1f, Prepositions

In the following sentences, enclose the complete prepositional phrases in parentheses and underline the prepositions.

For example: I walked (<u>to</u> the grocery, the fruit stand, and the bank).

1. On the move since dawn, the hikers had advanced twenty miles by lunchtime.

2. Sara finished three of the four essay questions quickly.

3. Chu's nieces and nephews danced around the room.

4. Bill saw his token roll into the street and disappear down a storm drain.

5. Forty-seven stories above the street, the falcons built their nest on one of the Chrysler Building's gargoyles.

6. After delivering the newspapers, Susan's hands were black with ink.

7. The river wound its way into town from the east.

8. In the excitement, I couldn't remember who came after me in the lineup.

9. "Singing in the Rain" is still one of Harlin's favorites.

10. Carol's hook shot bounced off the rim just after the buzzer sounded.

GRAM 1g, Conjunctions

In the following sentences, enclose the conjunction-containing clauses in parentheses. Then underline the conjunctions and label them as coordinating (COORD), subordinating (SUB), or correlative (CORREL).

For example: (If I had more money), I would replace my old car. (SUB)

1. I went to the store before Sushmito arrived.

2. It rained all night, so the tournament was postponed.

3. I like to fish even though I don't catch anything most days.

4. Although Melville's *Moby Dick* is a great book, there are some chapters that are slow reading.

5. Professor Pham asked us not only to compare and contrast Melville and Thoreau, but also to use one or more of their works to support our points.

6. As the sun rose over Lake Mead, the water became faceted with dancing white light.

7. Outside the pueblo it was hot and windy, but inside it was cool and quiet.

8. My grandfather used to say, "It's time to either cut bait or fish."

9. Rich and Gary, when they saw the long line for tickets, decided to go home and watch the game on television.

10. She disliked the medicine more than I.

GRAM 2a, Subjects

For each sentence that follows, underline the complete subject in the main clause.

For example: <u>Why anybody would live anyplace other than Texas</u> was a mystery to Annie.

1. My dog sleeps so much that my roommate thinks she's a stuffed animal.

2. Ly's enthusiasm for our annual reunion is infectious.

3. Joan's track and swimming talents earned her a scholarship.

4. Calculus 201 and Chemistry 137 have kept me extremely busy this semester.

5. The university has five libraries.

6. Riding the noisy IRT express train to school ensures that I am completely awake by the time I get off at 116th Street.

7. Branagh's remakes of *Henry V* and *Much Ado* have brought Shakespeare to new audiences.

8. There are many ways to define success.

9. Rain, rain, and more rain brought the Mississippi and its many tributaries to record levels in 1993.

10. The debate over national health care has raised many difficult questions.

GRAM 2b, Predicates

Underline the complete predicate in each of the following sentences.
For example: I work in Enrico's Deli from 8 to 11 weeknights.

1. Smoking is expensive and addictive.

2. Juan believed that his studies were a worthwhile investment.

3. Melissa's research paper explored the differences between personal debt and the national debt.

4. Gwen is the oldest of five children.

5. Bill and Ted cooked dinner together most nights.

6. Cronston Avenue ends just beyond Avenue M.

7. Lions sleep during much of the day.

8. Raoulito was happy he had backed up his hard disk when it crashed only a day later.

9. Nevin was shocked to find it harder to get a driver's license than purchase a gun.

10. Though Eliza lived on the sixth floor, she created a garden of tomatoes, lettuce, onions, and herbs by planting in window boxes.

GRAM 3b, Verbals

In the following sentences, underline the verbals and verbal phrases. Then identify their type as gerund (GER), infinitive (INF), past participle (PAST PART), or present participle (PRES PART).

For example: <u>Comparing Fred Astaire and Michael Jackson as dancers and singers</u> would be interesting. (PRES PART)

1. I love running because it requires so little equipment.

2. Pacing yourself during an exam is crucial.

3. The drummer playing the timbales is my cousin.

4. The Continental Army, faced with many hardships, managed to defeat the better trained and equipped British.

5. To conduct good science requires first, good training; second, good insight; and third, great effort.

6. Shooting the jumper in basketball is a lot easier when you plant both feet firmly before leaping.

7. The bird singing in the top of that tamarack is a wood thrush.

8. My grandmother always urged me to believe in myself.

9. Feeling the wind come up suddenly, Maggie suspected that a thunderstorm was approaching.

10. Stretching out before running is increasingly important as you age, especially to prevent injuries.

GRAM 4, Clauses

Underline and label the adjective (relative) clauses (ADJ CLS), adverb clauses (ADV CLS), and noun clauses (NOUN CLS) in the following sentences.

For example: The fish <u>that live in our lake</u> have been reduced in number recently by an increase in the cormorant population. (ADJ CLS)

1. When I saw Roger, who was just returning from a trip, he told me he would be playing softball with us this Saturday.

2. Ceilia painted her house purple because it was her favorite color.

3. If you hit or tip a ball foul and you already have two strikes, the count remains unchanged.

4. He hoped his contribution to the charity would benefit whoever was most in need.

5. After losing three games straight, the team was ebullient when it beat the undefeated first place team.

6. At the party on the night before she left for college, everyone wished Sumru well.

7. My motorcycle was magnificent when it ran and a great frustration the rest of the time.

8. Milo's family came over after they finished their dinner.

9. He knew a good deal when he saw it.

10. Our school's library, which was built in 1883, is a fine example of H. H. Richardson's work.

GRAM 5, Types of Sentences

Classify each of the following sentences by type: simple, compound, complex, or compound-complex.

For example: I reeled the fish in, and Bill netted it. (compound)

1. Though ordinary ink may look black, it also contains red pigment.

2. Fred likes to read in bed.

3. *The Grapes of Wrath* and *Of Mice and Men* are examples of books more acclaimed popularly than critically.

4. After scooping ice cream all summer, my right arm was so strong that I could beat my older brother in arm wrestling, and my left arm looked so withered to me that it seemed almost vestigial, like the forelegs of *Tyrannosaurus rex.*

5. Though it may sound odd, I swim in the winter and ski in the summer.

6. I read the book and wrote my analysis all in one day.

7. Antonia went from meeting to meeting until three o'clock, and then she caught a cab to the airport for her four o'clock flight.

8. She saved her money until she had enough to buy a laptop computer.

9. I repainted our room before my roommate returned from spring break, and all he could say when he saw it was that I must be color-blind.

10. Though there is much strife in the world, I maintain my optimism because I do not believe in types of people, only individuals.

Chapter 4

ESL BASICS

AN IMPORTANT REMINDER FOR STUDENTS: As noted in this exercise book's Preface, because of the flexibility of the English language there may be more than one way to correct the errors in each exercise; this is particularly true in this chapter. If you have any questions about your answers versus the ones supplied in the Selected Answers section, please ask your instructor. Very likely there will be other students with the same or similar questions.

ESL 1a, Modals

Correct the use of modal auxiliaries in the following sentences.

For example: Nick will not to swim in the lake with us.

Correction: Nick will not swim in the lake with us.

1. In one hour I be done.

2. You will to see me there tonight.

3. I should can finish this novel before class.

4. We cannot to come to the party.

5. When I was growing up, my family will usually take a trip in the summer.

6. Elly can is knowing how to operate the slide projector.

7. In ten minutes the eggs be ready.

8. Rizal can sings very well.

9. I can have to leave early.

10. He must cleaning up before he can go.

ESL 1b, Perfect Tenses

Correct the use of perfect tenses in the following sentences.

For example: She have found a nice new apartment.

Correction: She has found a nice new apartment.

1. They have travel too much this year to want to go on another trip soon.

2. We has expecting you yesterday.

3. Bill goes to the movies frequently; he will have saw that one already.

4. Chioë had sang in the choir for three years before she was chosen to be its director.

5. Suzanne have brung me flowers every year on my birthday.

6. The newspapers has watched the new president closely.

7. As of next spring, our organization will had support the children's hospital for twenty-five years.

8. I have drove on this road before.

9. They has gave Paulus an award two years in a row now.

10. She have raised a child even while enrolled in school.

ESL 1c, Progressive Tenses

Correct the use of progressive tenses in the following sentences.

For example: Lola been coming here every day.

Correction: Lola has been coming here every day.

1. John seeing Reno for the first time.

2. Sheila are giving her friends dancing lessons.

3. The ozone layer been thinning because of the release of CFCs.

4. Han is being happy today.

5. Sanga had be thinking calculus was easy until he took the midterm exam.

6. Jason is gone to the new Mamet play tomorrow night.

7. They will working on the scenery this afternoon.

8. By the time Mr. Tottle retires next year, he will been teaching at NBHS for thirty-eight years.

9. They be discussing Iris Dement's newest record album.

10. Anita been cooking her favorite dinner all afternoon.

ESL 1d, Passive Voice 1
Correct the use of the passive voice in the following sentences.
For example: The siren was heared by everyone on the street.
Correction: The siren was heard by everyone on the street.

1. The NHL championship was winned by Montreal this year.

2. Africa is visit by many Americans.

3. We were sitted by the hostess.

4. Many books is now published only in paperback.

5. Every student are expected to do well in his or her studies.

6. Many issues is discuss by the president's cabinet.

7. John were racked by the flu.

8. The national anthem was singed by Placido Domingo.

9. My pants were burnt when I ironed with the temperature too high.

10. The night course were added because many people couldn't attend during the day.

ESL 1d, Passive Voice 2
Rewrite the following passive voice sentences in the active voice.
For example: The siren was heard by everyone on the street.
Correction: Everyone on the street heard the siren.

1. My backpack was lost yesterday by Terusuke.

2. The Marine Works fountain is seen by many commuters every day.

3. *Carmen* was written by Bizet.

4. Reading is enjoyed by many people.

5. Money was scrupulously saved by my parents.

6. A good time was had by everyone.

7. Affordable housing was spoken about by the City Council at every meeting.

8. The satellite was boosted into geostationary orbit by the shuttle *Endeavor*.

9. The crowd was thrilled by Eminem's performance.

10. *Walden* was written by Henry David Thoreau during the period 1845–54.

ESL 1e, Two-Word Verbs
Correct the two-word verbs in the following sentences.
For example: Phil came a helpful article across.
Correction: Phil came across a helpful article.

1. Where's the newspaper? Oh, John threw away it?

2. The teacher called the student on.

3. Because of the extensive fire damage, the Fire Marshal ordered the building's owners to tear down it.

4. Simone heard her best friend from.

5. Why doesn't he pick someone on his own size?

6. The aspirin helped me get the cold over.

7. When you are in Santa Fe, don't forget to look up me.

8. Look my cat after while I am away.

9. The TV is too loud; please turn down it.

10. My dad learned that smoking was unhealthy, so he gave up it.

ESL 1f, Verbals

Correct the verbals in the following sentences.
For example: His father cautioned him using the crosswalk always.
Correction: His father cautioned him to use the crosswalk always.

1. They agreed come over here before the game.

2. Josef misses himself to eat home-cooked meals.

3. The boss permitted to take time off when my sister was married.

4. I imagine to fly is wonderful.

5. When I finish to eat, I'll read to you.

6. Please think about to save money for college.

7. Eriq is beginning sounding good on the piano.

8. Sam manages living well on a modest income.

9. Otto's parents invited me come with them to the show.

10. My best friend suggested to see the school's career counselors be-
    fore going to the interview.

ESL 2a–c, Count and Noncount Nouns 1

Correct the use of count and noncount nouns in the following sentences.

For example: John bought two beefs at the butcher.
Correction: John bought two pounds of beef at the butcher.

1. Gordon knows many local history.

2. How many breads did Orlo ask us to pick up?

3. Howard used two hundred pails of sands to build his huge sand castle.

4. Guadalupe said much machines are built there.

5. Don't put too many salt in the soup!

6. We received many, many snows here last winter.

7. My car used only 7 gallons of gasolines for the 300-mile trip.

8. An information can be stored in a computer.

9. The United States mixes much cultures.

10. My grandfather and I cooked 14 pound of tomato.

ESL 2a–c, Count and Noncount Nouns 2

Correct the use of count and noncount nouns in the following sentences.

For example: Sally didn't have enough quarter for the parking meter.
Correction: Sally didn't have enough quarters for the parking meter.

1. Gianni lost his cashes through a hole in his pocket.

2. Their new furnitures are beautiful.

3. Are there much students in your history class?

4. Is Karen still looking for the place to live?

5. The poet read her pieces with a lot of confidences.

6. How many rain fell here last month?

7. For this class there is a lot of book.

8. She said she would be here in two minute.

9. There is not much times before our mid-term exam.

10. I read that everyone should drink six glass of water every day.

ESL 2c–d, Articles

Correct the use of articles (definite, indefinite) in the following sentences. In some instances the correction may involve deleting the article. For example: I moved to United States to find the good job with a fair pay.

Correction: I moved to the United States to find a good job with fair pay.

1. Hour ago he left for the office.

2. A president is the former governor of Texas.

3. When she finishes the high school she wants to travel before finding an employment.

4. It was an hot day so we went to a beach.

5. She worked for the General Electric before joining an Intel.

6. Please pick me up pound of the coffee when you're at the market.

7. The Harry Connick, Jr. plays a piano and sings too.

8. Vietnam War still seems very recent to me.

9. The Honorable Judge Hotalling presided at hearing.

10. Bring towel and swimming suit to the party.

ESL 2d, Definite Article

Correct the use of the definite article in the following sentences.
For example: I moved to the Chicago when I was seven years old.
Correction: I moved to Chicago when I was seven years old.

1. [To the waiter:] May I have the ketchup please?

   [Later, when it's already on the table:] Please pass some ketchup.

2. Mount Katahdin is highest peak in Maine.

3. I saw professor who won Nobel Prize last year.

4. The hockey is very popular here.

5. I saw the Bob walking down the hall just a minute ago.

6. I arrive at the work by 8 a.m. every day.

7. After graduating, Francine was hired by the NASA.

8. Dora did not sing loudly, but her voice was best in the chorus.

9. I read last week that the calcium is important in your diet.

10. Montana is "A Big Sky State."

ESL 3a, Cumulative Adjectives

Correct the word order of the adjectives in the following items.
For example: Réal lives in a brown big house.
Correction: Réal lives in a big brown house.

1. a pearl white long necklace

2. my new first bicycle

3. square five small buildings

4. a brick ancient fireplace

5. triangular large seven windows

6. a nineteenth-century elegant waltz

7. a wooden white fence

8. the German most knowledgeable jurist

9. some small older cabs

10. the hottest summer five days

ESL 3b, Present and Past Participles

Correct the following sentences by changing past and present participles as necessary.

For example: The NBA finals are always excited.

Correction: The NBA finals are always exciting.

1. Lola found the novel's ending surprised.

2. The winter winds here are very dried.

3. Sofia found organic chemistry fascinated.

4. Jackie's remarks annoying me.

5. The kitchen scene in *Jurassic Park* was frightened.

6. Many visitors find the highways around Los Angeles confused.

7. The ocean water refreshing me.

8. Jean saw depressed similarities in the history of the 1930s and the 1990s.

9. I found Pacino's performance engaged.

10. Our hike into a strong wind all day left us exhausting.

ESL 3c, Adverbs

Correct the placement of adverbs in the following sentences.

For example: The food there always is good.

Correction: The food there is always good.

1. The president addresses traditionally the Congress in January.

2. There seems never to be enough time.

3. My older sister always is helpful.

4. I drove enough fast to get to work on time.

5. Ving went typically to the museum with his father.

6. Peter gave happily his present to his mother.

7. After the rainshower my clothes were enough wet to be wrung.

8. My dentist fails never to remind me to floss as well as brush.

9. John mailed early his package.

10. When she drove, she was focused extremely.

ESL 4a–c, Prepositions 1

Correct the use of prepositions in the following sentences.
For example: I prefer to travel in train rather than in plane.
Correction: I prefer to travel by train rather than by plane.

1. I went the movies nearly every week.

2. Francesca reads on the newspaper to improve her English.

3. When we first moved at Toronto, I missed Hong Kong very much.

4. Sari shops the grocery store everyday.

5. After his Fulbright in Sardinia, New England looked at very green to him.

6. Doug told me he works on his uncle's store.

7. Though I had read Shakespeare in translation before coming to the States, I am finding it entirely new for English.

8. The 107 bus stops at here at quarter past and quarter of the hour.

9. Sergei finished his story by time for class.

10. I would like to go the museum this Friday.

ESL 4d–f, Prepositions 2

Correct the use of prepositions in the following sentences.
For example: We called off our picnic because rain.
Correction: We called off our picnic because of rain.

1. Frederico was aware on the problem.

2. My brother's new glasses are for to read.

3. I walked as far Main Street before discovering that I had left my wallet at home.

4. How much is that equal of in dollars?

5. I like to paint as to well draw.

6. Due fog, the airport was closed.

7. "Come along me," called Gisela to Dave.

8. Omar was very proud for his diploma.

9. Addition to this book, you'll need that one.

10. Paul said, "After to exercise, stretch out and then shower."

ESL 5a–b, Omitted Verbs and Subjects

Correct the following sentences by ensuring that each clause has one subject and that linking verbs are present when needed.

For example: My house, which was built in 1922, it has many architectural details not found in newer houses.

Correction: My house, which was built in 1922, has many architectural details not found in newer houses.

1. My school has three libraries. Will begin construction of a fourth soon.

2. Dirk's whole family very amusing.

3. The baseball league, it begins its season next week.

4. This reading assignment very long.

5. The cicadas in the trees in my neighborhood they sing all day.

6. If clichés not true, why are they so often repeated?

7. My Great Uncle Tom, who loved to invent things, he was always fun to visit.

8. Dan's notebook, containing all his laboratory notes, it has been missing since yesterday.

9. My dinner, left too long in the oven, it became a black brick un-recognizable as food.

10. Our team won both games last week. Won last weekend, too.

ESL 5c, Expletives

Correct the use of expletives and verb agreement in the following sentences.

For example: Is a beautiful day today.
Correction: It is a beautiful day today.

1. There is three interstate highways into downtown Atlanta.

2. Here is my top choices for the position.

3. Here are the best recipe I have for turkey stuffing.

4. Is unlikely to rain when the sky is so clear.

5. There have many golf courses in Chittenden County.

6. Though the park is crowded, is still fun to be here.

7. She said there was two puppies for sale.

8. There is three bodegas on my block.

9. There are much speculation about why the dinosaurs disappeared.

10. Is true he won't run for another term as mayor?

ESL 6b, Questions with Who, Whom, and What

Correct the word order and helping verbs in the following questions containing *who*, *whom*, and *what*.

For example: What birds to migrate cause?
Correction: What causes birds to migrate?

1. Who are coming to dinner?

2. What congressional gridlock create?

3. Whom the president nominated?

4. Who today's mail brings in?

5. What the committee do?

6. Who is believing that explanation?

7. To who they sent the package?

8. What tides and currents in the ocean create?

9. Who take the bus to school?

10. What Murray listens to on the radio?

ESL 6c, Indirect Questions

For each sentence, find the indirect question and rewrite it as a direct question.

For example: I don't know what time she's planning to arrive.

Answer: What time is she planning to arrive?

1. The proposal is unclear about how they will finance the new day-care center.

2. He thought he knew which astronomer first identified and named M31.

3. My grandmother explained why my family came to this country in 1848.

4. She saw where the smoke was coming from.

5. Gena wonders how the U.S. Congress differs from the British Parliament.

6. I wasn't sure when Cassius Clay changed his name to Muhammad Ali.

7. The engineers investigated how gravity affected the growth of crystals.

8. Robert didn't know when we could visit the Dow Planetarium in Montreal.

9. I would like to know what makes a good bus driver.

10. Pita asked me what I would give her for her birthday.

ESL 6c, Indirect Questions

Correct the following indirect questions by using proper word order and verbs.

For example: The lead story traced how has drug use changed in the last decade.

Correction: The lead story traced how drug use has changed in the last decade.

1. He asked me are you coming or not.

2. Rupert wasn't sure when did the Battle of Hastings occur.

3. We tried to see where did the rocket go.

4. The committee researched why has the cost of education outpaced inflation in the last ten years.

5. Everice asked do you enjoy playing racquetball.

6. The reporter asked when will we see the mayor's new budget.

7. I don't understand how does this lock work.

8. My nephew wondered did I want to go to the park with him.

9. Tamara is not sure will you like pistachio ice cream.

10. I asked myself how can he be so late?

ESL 6d, Reported Speech

For the following sentences, rewrite the direct quotations as reported speech and the reported speech as direct quotation.

Reported: He said he'd been looking forward to meeting my family for a long time.

Direct: He said, "I've been looking forward to meeting your family for a long time."

1. "I love zucchini," said Nino, "almost as much as I love peppers."

2. Bob told me that he was working in the library five nights per week.

3. "Roger has played a faltering but passionate cello for years," Erin opined with a grin.

4. Mary announced that she would be running in the Bay to the Breakers race this year.

5. "Wait for the third quarter results," said the company spokesperson.

6. Annika observed that she had not seen many men in bikinis in beer commercials.

7. "Will the economy improve this year, Mr. Greenspan?" the anxious Senate Finance Committee member asked.

8. The reporter asked the candidate whether or not she would vote for House Resolution 143.

9. "I may not have the money to travel home for Thanksgiving this year," Willy told me.

10. Whenever my grandmother found me working late, she would tell me that two hours at night were worth one hour in the morning.

ESL 6e, Conditional Sentences

Correct the verbs in the following conditional sentences.
For example: When air warms, it will rise.
Correction: When air warms, it rises.

1. If he sees a shooting star, he will make a wish.

2. If you practice enough, you could join a band.

3. If I had practiced more, I may have my own band.

4. Wherever Fleetwood Mac performed last year, they find big audiences.

5. If Al Gore had been elected, what changes would he make?

6. If you were the laboratory's teaching assistant, what will you do?

7. Whenever she has trouble sleeping, she will drink some warm milk and go right back to bed.

8. If we get lost on the way to the airport, we would miss our plane.

9. When I exercise at least three days per week, my back will never bother me.

10. Unless I hear from him today, I am assuming he is coming tomorrow.

Chapter 5

SENTENCES

SENT 1, Parallelism
Rewrite the following sentences to improve their parallel structure.
For example: Planes and trains are usually on time, and buses are, too.
Correction: Planes, trains, and buses are all usually on time.

1. We will see Rufus on Tuesday, and then Wednesday we are going to see Tito.

2. Though he could not swim, a life jacket was something he would not wear.

3. El Niño has remained active in the Pacific, and the rain continues to fall.

4. Congress does not think enough about the individual citizen, and it forgets about personal responsibility.

5. As the sun rose, the moon was setting.

6. Our team is well prepared and has great equipment; our coach too is excellent, and we've had a lot of practices.

7. I see a great future ahead, while in the past our record has been admirable.

8. He wanted to be on the stage, but he knew neither how to act nor singing.

9. Is it better to stand fast on environmental policy than having a compromise in order to save jobs?

10. At the local Kwik-Gas she is the manager, and she is also our class valedictorian.

SENT 2, Misplaced and Dangling Modifiers

Rewrite the following sentences to eliminate the misplaced and dangling modifiers.

For example: Jim could see the fish jumping from the campsite.

Correction: From the campsite Jim could see the fish jumping.

1. Don returned the tools to Phil covered with grease.

2. Threatened with extinction, the EPA wrote new rules for the spotted owl.

3. I saw him on the walkway painted green.

4. Young and inexperienced jobs were few and far between Jim discovered.

5. I wrote directions for my friend to the house.

6. Prized by many, Leon won the award.

7. I saw a big grouper with my mask and snorkel on.

8. It was so hot that I watched Elizabeth Taylor and Richard Burton dressed only in my shorts in *Who's Afraid of Virginia Woolf.*

9. I gave Dulla a book in the library written by Faulkner.

10. I could see Stonehenge coming over the hill.

SENT 3a–c, Shifts 1

Correct the inappropriate shifts in person, number, tense, or mood in the following sentences. Indicate the type of shift you are correcting. For example: I played basketball at the Y for years. I like their courts.
Correction: I played basketball at the Y for years. I liked their courts.
(tense shift)

1. The United Nations' membership has grown steadily, and they add one or more new members nearly every year.

2. When I study, I will usually work for at least three hours.

3. Once people swim in this lake, especially in August, you never want to swim anywhere else.

4. My father works for 42 years; he retired last month.

5. I will take the train to St. Louis; let's go on the 10:37 train.

6. Although one prepared for the storm, I was nonetheless scared by its ferocity.

7. It is crucial to study regularly and don't get behind.

8. Denise reminded me to be sure to come early so you could get a good seat.

9. When I asked Nando what the difference was between handball and team handball, he says he doesn't know.

10. I remembered his advice that one has to swing smoothly in order to hit well.

SENT 3d–g, Shifts 2

Correct the inappropriate shifts in subject, voice, quotation (direct versus indirect), tone, style, or point of view in the following sentences. Indicate the type of shift you are correcting.

For example: I told them to come on over if you want to learn the new rhythms.

Correction: I told them, "Come on over if you want to learn the new rhythms." (quotation shift)

1. I went to the new restaurant on Elm Street, and we enjoyed the meal.

2. Recycling newsprint requires extensive sophisticated processing, such as the de-inking of paper and the handling of the heavy metals extracted—no piece of cake.

3. Arlene said that she had read an interesting story in the *San Francisco Chronicle* and you should read it too.

4. Broken down, we sat until the Transit Authority sent a replacement bus.

5. The school's main entrance was an imposing series of granite steps and landings leading up to a pair of great carved oak doors. The hallways were dark and long.

6. When we met at the Java Joint, the film was our main topic of discussion.

7. The trees lining the avenue created a leafy canopy overhead that looked like a green river running through the heart of the city.

8. The folks at the FDA have the important task of regulating the composition and safe use of food and drugs.

9. The point of diminishing returns was approached as Congress continued to modify the budget.

10. If someone wants to learn to read faster and better, it can be done through practice.

SENT 4a, Irrelevant Detail

Edit the following sentences to eliminate irrelevant detail.

For example: The author's second novel, nearly four hundred pages long, did not receive the widespread acclaim of her first.

Correction: The author's second novel did not receive the widespread acclaim of her first.

1. Marx said that religion is the opium of the people, which is, I think, a strong opinion.

2. Charles Dickens, who died in 1870, was a prolific author, working on up to three novels concurrently.

3. In the last six months our newly-elected Republican president, when not discussing the budget, has announced during White House press briefings plans to elevate several governmental posts to the rank of cabinet officer.

4. Last Thanksgiving Chuck walked to and from the museum where he saw the Matisse retrospective.

5. The interstate highway system, originally constructed for reasons of national security, is now badly in need of extensive rebuilding.

6. Whenever the wind blows from the north, which is actually quite often, you can hear the windows in our apartment whistle.

7. The area between the Tigris and Euphrates rivers, home many years ago to the Akkadians and the Amorites, is known as "the cradle of civilization."

8. Sponsored each year by a number of local organizations, our class trip to the U.N. was fascinating.

9. My brother, who loves to read, was just elected captain of the basketball team.

10. When I read Carey's *The Tax Inspector* it was during finals week and I enjoyed it.

SENT 4b, Mixed or Illogical Constructions

Edit the following sentences to eliminate mixed or illogical constructions.

For example: The reason why the baby cried is because her diaper needed changing.

Correction: The baby cried because her diaper needed changing.

1. He said that the new bridge won't increase nobody's taxes.

2. They chatted like two birds until they ran out of steam.

3. The triple chocolate cake, my favorite recipe, was always delicious.

4. My brother wrote me a letter last week and I read them two or three times over.

5. I don't know nothing about Wagner's opera *Parsifal*.

6. Beginning after lunch, the wind blew all day.

7. The coach gave us six new plays that was designed to confuse their defense.

8. Martin Luther King, Jr., his speeches powerful, always captured the attention of his audiences.

9. On Green Up Day my whole class went to Central Park's playground and cleaned them up.

10. The reason abortion is such a contentious issue is because many people have differing views that they are absolutely sure are correct.

SENT 5a, Subordination

Using subordination, rewrite each set of short sentences as one sentence. For example: The day was dreary. We went fishing anyway.
Rewritten: Although the day was dreary, we went fishing anyway.

1. Bill and Metsa have dated for five years. They started in high school. They think they will get married next year.

2. Allan Iverson is fast. He plays both offense and defense well. He can play both because of his speed.

3. Our university library has over one million volumes. It covers most areas of information in depth. It also has information that is up-to-date. I do most of my research there.

4. Heat the sauce over a low flame. Stir constantly. Be sure that the butter does not brown.

5. The Statue of Liberty once again looks beautiful. It was a gift of the French people. It was dedicated in 1886. It was restored for its centennial. It is more than one hundred years old.

6. I meet Sala for lunch every Friday. I enjoy talking with her.

7. Kim studied all weekend for the exam. He was tired. He did well on the exam on Monday.

8. The sun was hot. The humidity was high. It had been this way for two weeks. John wouldn't even play baseball.

9. My mother is a Stones fan. My father is a Beatles fan. They are both diehards. They still argue over which group is better. I have to listen to these childish discussions.

10. My sister is tall. She is strong. She is a team player. She was elected captain of the volleyball team.

SENT 5c, Coordination

Using coordination, rewrite each set of short sentences as one sentence.

For example: The U.S. economy is very complex. The Federal Reserve Board has a difficult job.

Rewritten: The U.S. economy is very complex, so the Federal Reserve Board has a difficult job.

1. I had a lot of reading to do every day. I did not watch television at all for months.

2. She agrees with many things Roberto tells her. She argues with him when she does not.

3. My great uncle does not smoke. He also does not drink.

4. He likes classical music. He also likes country and western.

5. This rain is good for people. It is filling the reservoirs.

6. At the heart of brewing is yeast. It converts sugars to alcohol and carbon dioxide.

7. We grow a garden every summer. We eat fresh vegetables every day.

8. I generally agree with Professor Tellman's theories. I am still unsure about some of his research.

9. I can take the 7:10 train. I can catch the 7:20 bus.

10. Copernicus used astronomical instruments that are very simple by modern standards. Copernicus changed our whole concept of humanity's place in the universe.

SENT 6a, Emphasis

Rewrite the following sentences placing the most important words or phrases at the beginning or end of the sentence.

For example: With politicians who happily confuse deficit reduction with debt reduction, what is the chance that the "Peace Dividend" is something we'll ever see?

Rewritten: With politicians who happily confuse deficit reduction with debt reduction, what is the chance we'll ever see a "Peace Dividend"?

1. Phil told me that Hogan's party was a great success once the band got going and everyone began to dance.

2. Not heeding a winter storm warning can be a grave mistake in New England.

3. When I first heard the plan I was thrilled, but now I'm not so sure.

4. Pedro's new job is challenging, so he's glad he took it.

5. *Carmen,* which Luis has seen eight times, is his favorite opera.

6. Erica was shocked by the calculation that $50,000 would be the cost of her college education.

7. The idea that love could overcome every obstacle was something Johanne believed.

8. In their discussions, the United Nations and NATO seemed almost paralyzed with uncertainty about how to best handle Bosnia.

9. The last editor of the *New Yorker*, Tina Brown, changed both the look and the content of the magazine.

10. A rattlesnake's bite is rarely fatal if the victim knows what to do.

SENT 6b, Logical Order

Rewrite each of the following sentences to improve its logical and/or climactic sequence.

For example: Franco passed the bar exam, studied hard, and was hired by a prestigious law firm.

Rewritten: Franco studied hard, passed the bar exam, and was hired by a prestigious law firm.

1. We arrived at the Grand Canyon, hiked to the Colorado River a mile below, and loaded our packs.

2. Boggs had an awful day when we were at Fenway; he struck out in the first, seventh, and fifth innings.

3. I like a movie if it has a good story, ends happily, and is well acted.

4. In the next three hours I need to dress to go out, shower and shave, and mow the lawn.

5. As I looked around the dimly lit attic, I saw dusty boxes, a complete human skeleton, and piles of old clothes.

6. After landing in Houston, Marty picked up his luggage, drove into the city, and rented a car.

7. The thunderstorm raced in—the hard rain driving, the explosive lightning crazing the landscape into a ghostly, crackling white, and the wind rising.

8. To set up a family budget first determine what, if any, you can spend, then what your income is, and last what your expenses are.

9. John began his research paper by reading on his topic, taking notes, and finding a topic.

10. I admire Matisse's fantastic sense of form and movement, his rich use of color, and his brush work.

SENT 6c, Active Voice

Rewrite the following sentences to change the active voice to the passive voice, or vice versa.

For example: Fresh peas were loved by Julie. (passive voice)
Rewritten: Julie loved fresh peas. (active voice)

1. Mosquitoes, black flies, and chiggers bit Paul on his canoe trip down the Allegash.

2. The ball was hit deep to center by Griffey.

3. A new puppy was bought by the family.

4. Everyone in our dorm celebrated Kurt's birthday.

5. I was called by Patrick as soon as he returned to Seattle.

6. By whom was *A River Runs through It* written?

7. Many immigrants were examined by the U.S. Naturalization Service at Ellis Island.

8. Angela was read *Goodnight Moon* by her parents as a child.

9. Now Angela reads *Goodnight Moon* to Rosauro every night.

10. Maya's report was praised by her boss.

SENT 7a, Sentence Variety 1

Rewrite the following sentences to eliminate the overuse of short, simple sentences.

For example: Darif had a great day. He was early for class. He got an A on his midterm. He received a birthday card from his parents.

Rewritten: Darif was early for class, got an A on his midterm, and received a birthday card from his parents—a great day.

1. It rained for a month. There was great flooding.

2. Vermont has a long winter. It seems shorter now that I ski.

3. My parents sang every Sunday in church for years. Last year they stopped. They miss it now.

4. Fly over any major U.S. city. Look out the plane's window. You will be shocked by the number of swimming pools you will see.

5. Anne gets up at 5 a.m. every day. She never misses her gymnastics practice.

6. A house has many main parts. It has a foundation. It has a frame. It has sheathing. It has internal systems, such as electricity and plumbing.

7. I heard Lazlo's newest album on the radio. It's another hit, I think.

8. Every morning I get up. I exercise. I shower and dress. I carpool to work.

9. Hume read an article about government waste. It made him feel

frustrated.

10. A new mall was proposed. It raised many questions. One of them

was whom would it benefit.

SENT 7b, Sentence Variety 2
Rewrite sentences A and B to begin with the structure indicated.
Given: Roland and Lynda walked in the park and forgot about
              all their cares for the evening.
Begin with a gerund:
Rewritten: Walking in the park was Roland and Lynda's way to forget about
              all their cares for the evening.

Sentence A: Roland and Lynda walked in the park and forgot about all

their cares for the evening.

1. Begin with an infinitive:

2. Begin with a participle:

3. Begin with a subordinate clause:

4. Begin with a coordinating conjunction:

5. Begin with a prepositional phrase:

Sentence B: Samuel de Champlain discovered a great freshwater lake, and claimed it for France to please the king in 1609.

6. Begin with an infinitive:

7. Begin with a participle:

8. Begin with a subordinate clause:

9. Begin with a coordinating conjunction:

10. Begin with a prepositional phrase:

Chapter 6

EDITING FOR GRAMMAR

EDIT 1a–d, Subject–Verb Agreement 1

Correct the errors in subject–verb agreement in the following sentences.
For example: The depth of all three ponds are unknown.
Correction: The depth of all three ponds is unknown.

1. The ticket, including dinner with dessert, a floor show, and dancing after, cost only twenty dollars.

2. The smell of the ripening apples and pears attract bees to the orchard.

3. Neither my parents nor my brother want to try my latest culinary triumph: cranberry-tofu meat loaf.

4. The House's minority makes their voices heard.

5. High tides and wind creates dangerous conditions along the coast.

6. Fourteen aunts, uncles, and cousins, except for Gramma Gump, was coming to our cookout.

7. The new library, though it had no windows, were bright and pleasant inside.

8. Six loaves of bread is not enough for this group.

9. Smith, Ruggles & Cleary have been practicing law for fifty years.

10. The House of Representatives are on summer recess.

EDIT 1e–l, Subject–Verb Agreement 2

Correct the errors in subject–verb agreement in the following sentences.

For example: He was the first of the thirteen batters who was struck
out by Clemens.

Correction: He was the first of the thirteen batters who were struck out by
Clemens.

1. Anyone who study regularly will do better in school and enjoy it more.

2. All the explanations is inadequate.

3. None of my classes meet before 10 a.m.

4. There is, on a regulation baseball team, nine players.

5. Politics both fascinate and repulse him.

6. Newspapers that covers controversial issues must work hard to be fair.

7. *Profiles in Courage* were written by John F. Kennedy.

8. One of his pairs of pants are ripped.

9. Whether privatization will result in more efficient services are de-
batable.

10. *Data* are the plural of *datum.*

EDIT 2a–b, Principal Parts of Irregular Verbs

Correct the misuse of irregular verbs in the following sentences.

For example: When the thunderstorm came through, it awakened me.

Correction: When the thunderstorm came through, it awoke me.

1. If you bent the pipe more, I think it will fit.

2. After John set down, he pulled out a book and dozed off.

3. Having took the subway for years, I was not easily startled by
unusual-looking passengers.

4. Paul took the dinner roast out at noon because it was froze.

5. Having digged the trench, the workers laid the new gas line.

6. I had wrote to him all summer, but he only replied with a single postcard.

7. When the bell rung, the lecturer began immediately.

8. Once the paintings were hanged, the artist relaxed and got ready for the opening.

9. Many flowers and wreaths are lain at the Vietnam Memorial every day.

10. It was his favorite sweatshirt, so he wore it even though it was tore.

EDIT 2c, Verb Tense

Rewrite the sentence provided in the verb tenses indicated.

For example: John and I often go to the movies together.

Present Perfect: *John and I have often gone to the movies together.*

I go to the All-Star Game every year.

1. Present Perfect:

2. Present Progressive:

3. Present Perfect Progressive:

4. Past:

5. Past Perfect:

6. Past Progressive:

7. Past Perfect Progressive:

8. Future:

9. Future Perfect:

10. Future Progressive:

11. Future Perfect Progressive:

EDIT 2e, Verb Mood

Write, in the parentheses provided, the mood of the underlined clause.
Then rewrite the sentence, inventing as necessary, to change the under-
lined clause to the mood indicated at the beginning of the second line.
For example:

(   )   <u>Come home after practice.</u>

INDICATIVE:

First fill in the mood of the underlined clause: (imperative). Second,
rewrite the sentence, changing the underlined clause to the mood listed
at the beginning of the second line ("INDICATIVE"). Thus, a completed
answer might look like this:

(imperative)   <u>Come home after practice.</u>

INDICATIVE: I will come home after practice.

1. (   ) Bob asked <u>that he come early today.</u>

   IMPERATIVE:

2. (   ) <u>If I were training harder,</u> I would be better prepared.

   INDICATIVE:

3. (   ) <u>Every night he reads until bedtime.</u>

   SUBJUNCTIVE:

4. (   ) Mary said, "<u>Hurry up or we'll miss the bus.</u>"

   INDICATIVE:

5. (   ) <u>I wished it were snowing,</u> but it was only raining.

   INDICATIVE:

6. (   ) Lili said <u>her voice was similar to Cheryl Crow's.</u>

   SUBJUNCTIVE:

7. (   ) Don asked <u>if the campers could settle down.</u>

   SUBJUNCTIVE:

8. (   ) Chris wished <u>he were able to work more often</u>
   <u>at Caspian</u>.
   INDICATIVE:

9. (   ) <u>If it were up to me</u>, I'd change the policy.
   INDICATIVE:

10. (   ) "<u>Don't forget to pick me up, Berto!</u>"
    SUBJUNCTIVE:

EDIT 2f, Active and Passive Voices
Rewrite each sentence changing its voice (that is, rewrite sentences in the passive voice in the active voice, and vice versa). Indicate the voice used in your rewritten sentence.
Example: *Star Trek* is loved by millions of Trekkies.
Rewritten: (active) Millions of Trekkies love *Star Trek*.

1. Jamal mailed the letters after lunch.

2. The dinner was cooked by Raoul.

3. Wallace Stegner wrote *Angle of Repose*.

4. Regina saw the Blue Line bus.

5. The World Series is watched by many people who rarely watch baseball otherwise.

6. The hills were set aglow by the summer sun.

7. Horseback riding demands subtle athleticism.

8. Our guide called the tallest redwood the "Mother of the Forest."

9. Their farm produces 10,000 pounds of milk each day.

10. Inline skates are often used by people in the park.

EDIT 3a, Pronoun Agreement

Correct the errors in pronoun-antecedent agreement in the following sentences.

For example: If someone calls, please tell them I'll call back in an hour.

The problem: *someone* is singular, *them* is plural. There are many possible solutions; here are two:

> If someone calls, please tell him or her I'll call back in an hour.
> (grammatically correct but somewhat awkward)

> If someone calls, please say I'll call back in an hour.
> (switch to the verb *say*, which doesn't require an indirect object such as *them*, *him*, or *her*.)

1. The faculty votes for their officers every October.

2. He needs to better train his dog Biff, which barks at the letter carrier every day.

3. Neither Mrs. Williams nor Mr. Williams remembered their birthday.

4. When Louisa and Hal come to visit, they always bring his and her dog.

5. Each player in the tournament took his turn at the table.

6. The orchestra will open their twenty-eighth season with tonight's performance.

7. Either you or your sister need to mow the lawn today.

8. Nicole's brother that served in the Navy is going to marry my sister.

9. My father and mother had his and her favorite dinner—fresh trout.

10. If someone liked *E.T.*, I think he will love *A.I.*

EDIT 3b, Pronoun Reference

Correct the vague or confusing pronoun references in the following sentences.

For example: Lisa told Joan that her car sounded as though it needed a tune up.

The problem: Whose car needs a tune up, Lisa's or Joan's? There are many possible solutions; here is one:

Lisa said, "Joan, your car sounds as though it needs a tune up."

1. Last night Adriano saw eight deer on the Charlotte-Hinesburg Road, which was unusual.

2. Professor Marilee Tecknor, who studies retroviruses and has isolated a new subclass, gave a lecture on them at our seminar.

3. Though I know that supply-side economics focuses on production, and demand-side economics emphasizes consumption, this has never helped me understand where my paycheck goes every week.

4. When the company demanded a cut in wages and benefits, they recommended a strike vote be taken.

5. When tours come through our town, they often stop at the Shelburne Museum, where you can see an extensive American folk art collection.

6. Santa Cruz County offers both the mountains and the ocean, so they rarely wish to move anywhere else.

7. The freeway was backed up all the way to the toll plaza, and it was unlikely to clear out for several hours.

8. Cormac McCarthy's *All the Pretty Horses* combines ample description with sparse dialog and it creates a sense of the lone horseman riding through the vast, southwestern landscape.

9. In the newspaper they said the show opens tomorrow.

10. Driving into Livonia on my last trip which is near Detroit, I ran out of gas.

EDIT 3c, Pronoun Case 1

Correct the pronoun case errors in the following sentences.
For example: The woman on the right is her.
Correction: The woman on the right is she.

1. Have you seen mine brother?

2. After taking the A train, Chuck and me went to the deli.

3. If it were up to Laura and I, we'd leave now.

4. The boss appreciated them working on Saturday night.

5. My sister said she would be going to visit our grandmother after visiting Susan and I.

6. Gloria and me are best friends.

7. Us winning the Tri-City Invitational made the whole school proud.

8. Her and me studied for the exam with Tom, Rico, and Zino.

9. The president of the student council is him.

10. Because the package was addressed to she and I, we did not wait for my brother to get home before opening it.

EDIT 3c–d, Pronoun Case 2

Correct the pronoun case errors in the following sentences.

For example: Fritz likes to swim more than me.

Correction: Fritz likes to swim more than I.

1. Professor Mbutuze asked Dave and I to participate in the experiment.

2. Despite all his campaigning, the *New York Times* reported that the incumbent was running stronger than him.

3. My sister, whom has incredibly acute hearing when it comes to the telephone, yelled out from the shower, "Who is that call for?"

4. With two runners on, Lana and I, our best hitter came to the plate.

5. The victory will go to whomever crosses the finish line first.

6. The registrar required Donna and she to submit transcripts for their summer work.

7. My brother and I are avid readers, but he hasn't read as many books as me this summer.

8. Because it was a tie, the prize was given to two runners, Phil and I.

9. I forget her name, but the Oscar for Best Actress went to whomever played the older Schlegel sister in *Howard's End*.

10. *For Whom the Bell Tolls* was written by who?

EDIT 4, Adjectives and Adverbs

Correct the errors in adjective and adverb usage in the following sentences.

For example: Josh can swim real fast.

Correction: Josh can swim really fast.

1. Laura grew more and more confidently as the semester progressed.

2. I think it's coldest today than yesterday.

3. The NRC is charged with monitoring this kind of nuclear safety issues.

4. He is doing good in pottery class.

5. With two of their starters on the disabled list, things look badly for the Seattle Mariners.

6. The steadily increase in sales before the holidays was offset by their declining steadily for the six months after the holidays.

7. After eating a $9 "Tub-o-Pop" at the movies, Sam was feeling badly.

8. Dirk read so quick that he finished the assignment a day before me.

9. The characters seemed happily engaged, but unhappily married.

10. Even though Elaine was a healthy thirty-four-year-old who had always eaten good, each Thanksgiving her grandmother said she looked a little thin.

EDIT 5, Sentence Fragments

Rewrite the following sentences to eliminate sentence fragments.
For example: He loves to fish. Also hunt and hike.
Correction: He loves to fish, hunt, and hike.

1. My little brother is 6' 2 ". And still growing.

2. My big brother Todd swam in high school. And dove in college.

3. While on vacation I read two books. Nicholas Evans's *The Horse Whisperer* and Frances Mayes's *Under the Tuscan Sun.*

4. Last night I saw Neville at the student union; Molly, too.

5. When I saw the Mona Lisa in person. I was, to be honest, disappointed.

6. The city jobs bill was stalled in the state legislature. Which is unfortunate.

7. Snappy replies on *Face the Nation* can win you votes. But do not constitute governing.

8. I saw most of my family over Thanksgiving. Anne, Michael, Kate, and Maggie.

9. Gertrude is my closest friend. Even though she moved to Prague.

10. After summer, I saw Jean very little. By winter, not at all.

EDIT 6, Comma Splices

Rewrite the following sentences to eliminate comma splices.

For example: I love to cook, I hate to diet.

Correction: I love to cook, but hate to diet.

1. The American Civil War was the earliest instance of modern warfare, many experts continue to believe.

2. Professor Gerson has a pleasantly acid sense of humor, he quipped that the term *European ally* is an oxymoron.

3. I practice conga one hour every day, this has helped me improve a lot in the last year.

4. Spring in San Francisco is cool, many visitors wished they had brought warmer clothes.

5. I am a business major, studying economics will give me a useful background.

6. Picasso's work has been classified into periods, perhaps best known is his Blue Period.

7. It was raining lightly, we set off on the hike anyway.

8. My roommate reported that my old sneakers had begun to move on their own, he said they were a violation of U.S. treaties banning the development of biological weapons.

9. I had never driven to San Jose before, I missed my exit from Route 85.

10. Kaitlin reads the newspaper every morning, she is much more knowledgeable about current affairs than I.

EDIT 6, Fused Sentences

Rewrite the following to eliminate fused sentences.

For example: Mariah was very physically fit she worked out five days a
week.

Correction: Mariah was very physically fit because she worked out five days
a week.

1. We took a cab to the theatre we saw *Show Boat*.

2. I hope Ben will come over and help me with my car I need to adjust the carburetor.

3. It rained for twenty days straight I felt like escaping to the desert.

4. I know what a typeface is I'm not quite sure what a font is.

5. The last U.S. space shuttle flight to Mir was made in 1999, since then all shuttle flights have been to the new International Space Station.

6. I saw Leah yesterday she looked great.

7. I think it's three o'clock do we have to leave now?

8. When I visited Nyla over the holidays, I met many of her high school friends they were very friendly.

9. Can you come here and taste this soup I need an opinion.

10. We trained the telescope to the south Saturn was clearly visible.

Chapter 7

WORD CHOICE

WORD 1, Eliminating Clutter

Rewrite each of the following wordy sentences to make them concise and direct.

Example: Good, clear instructions eliminate, I think, a lot of possible confusion later.

Rewritten: Clear instructions eliminate later confusion.

1. I'd say that Tom was basically a point guard that can, when he's got to, play center.

2. I thought that the test was really hard on account of the fact that we had to know in essence everything from the whole semester.

3. Due to the fact that there was bad weather in Atlanta, Bill's two brothers, who were flying, were delayed and we had to wait at the airport for them for five hours.

4. The school band, which it seems to me obviously hadn't practiced enough, couldn't even play the national anthem without mistakes.

5. Can you explain why it is that schools of fish, which live in the water, and flocks of birds that fly in the air, move as a single group with similar coordinated motions?

6. The trees on my street, which are of three different types, all change color in fall at what I would estimate to be the very same time.

7. The governor, who was popular and who was already serving his third term in office, was given yet another vote of confidence at the polls by the voting populace at election time.

8. In spite of the fact that Orlo, who is conductor of our orchestra, was late, the concert began virtually on time.

9. While everyone's point of view, and ideas, and feelings, must be taken into account and assessed carefully and thoughtfully, it seems to me that in the end the president is kind of charged with the task of leading rather than evaluating.

10. Red Barber for all intents and purposes was a great reporter of sporting news for the simple reason that he was spare with his use of words, and he will long be remembered for that.

WORD 2a, Denotation

Replace the italicized word—used incorrectly—in each of the following sentences with a word that denotes the correct meaning. Then identify the part of speech and write a short definition for both the incorrect and correct words. Consult a dictionary if necessary.

Example: Albert Einstein's work was *ingenuous*.

Answer: Albert Einstein's work was ingenious.
 ingenuous: (adj) naive
 ingenious: (adj) clever and inventive

1. What are the *affects* of the new spending bill?

2. Even if you disagree strongly with him, please be *civic*.

3. Emile was a *vociferous* reader.

4. Sex education has helped many teenagers get factual information on *venerable* diseases.

5. Paul, carried away by the emotional appeal of his own argument, went off on a *tangible*.

6. In an effort to keep the peace talks going, the U.S. ambassador *shuffled* between the countries in contention.

7. This apartment is cold because its walls have no *isolation*.

8. My new car uses almost 50 percent less fuel than my old one; its engine is much more *proficient*.

9. The facilitator successfully *meditated* the dispute.

10. George is *libel* to come in here at any moment.

WORD 2c, General versus Specific Words

For each general word in the list, provide a specific example.

Example: emotions: happiness

1. transportation:

2. foods:

3. vegetables:

4. seasons:

5. holidays:

6. colors:

7. metals:

8. trees:

9. music:

10. birds:

WORD 2c, Abstract versus Concrete Words

Identify each word in the following list as either abstract or concrete.

Example: emotions: abstract

1. pretty:

2. justice:

3. leaves:

4. blue:

5. stars:

6. wood:

7. fast:

8. cake:

9. truth:

10. shoes:

11. paper:

12. bright:

13. fun:

14. rock:

15. tall:

16. new:

17. slippery:

18. wind:

19. music:

20. juice:

WORD 2d, Idioms

Correct the misuse of prepositions in the following sentences containing idiomatic expressions.

Example: I am concerned for your attitude.
Correction: I am concerned with your attitude.

1. The committee agreed with the plan.

2. Frieda left early so that she would be sure and get a good seat.

3. My niece insisted that Jell-O was superior than pudding.

4. Though we arrived early, we still had to wait on line.

5. The coach gave me some extra tips to help me try and improve my shot.

6. Their route was different than ours.

7. The House of Representatives concurred with the Senate's resolution.

8. Jazz is Hector's favorite type of a music.

9. When dancing with a partner, try not to vary to the beat.

10. Houston Street is parallel from Canal.

WORD 3a–b, Appropriate Formality

Rewrite each of the following sentences, substituting for the italicized word or phrase a more formal expression.

Example: Jagdish *took off* after work.
Answer: Jagdish left after work.

1. Reggie *couldn't stand* their new album.

2. Bryan *can't* come today.

3. The show was *awesome.*

4. Collecting stamps was Phil's *thing.*

5. If I have time, *I'll catch a bite* with you at noon.

6. What *stuff* did Professor Higgins *talk about* today?

7. K.C. said, *"Don't dis your sis."*

8. When *I'm done, I'm gonna cruise for* Ridley's.

9. Rickie decided *to hang* in the library *til* I finished.

10. Ozzie *shot the breeze* with Harriet on the porch.

WORD 4, Bias in Writing

Rewrite each of the following sentences to eliminate sexist terminology.

Example: Suzanne Porter was the anchorman on our local news.
Answer: *Suzanne Porter was the anchor on our local news.*

1. Our forefathers showed great courage to leave their homelands and voyage to a new and often little-known country.

2. The president was swamped with questions from the newsmen.

3. The writing course was tailored to freshmen students.

4. Who's chairman of that Senate subcommittee?

5. Of all creatures on the planet, man is the most intelligent and the most destructive.

6. My bag is so heavy that I hope the hotel has a bellboy.

7. My sister-in-law is a policeman.

8. The job was so big that Laura was not sure our department had enough manpower to complete the work on time.

9. The plane was full and the stewardesses had to hustle throughout the flight.

10. All the firemen in my town are volunteers.

WORD 5, The Dictionary

Use your dictionary to answer the following questions.

1. How many syllables are in *oblivious* and *obnoxious*? Write out both words and mark the syllable breaks.

2. Define *marathon* and explain the origin of the word.

3. What is the etymology of the word *lens*? What type of lens best exemplifies this origin?

4. What is the origin of the word *frankfurter*?

5. How many syllables are in *scrupulous*? Write out the word and mark the syllable breaks.

6. Check the etymology of the word *bait*. You will find that it is a particular form of a related word that is also found in English. What is that other word?

7. What are the two meanings of the noun *chamois*? What are the variant spellings of this word?

8. What is the origin of the name of the game *hop-scotch*?

9. How has the word *apron* changed over time? (Hint: What is faulty separation?) Give a similar word that did not undergo this same change.

10. What is it that makes a *March hare* mad?

WORD 6, The Thesaurus

For each word given use a thesaurus to find five or more synonyms and at least one antonym. Indicate the part of speech for your entries.

Example: probe

Answer: noun: investigation; inquiry; examination; exploration; research; scrutiny; study
             verb: explore; delve; dig; penetrate
             antonym: (noun) cover-up

1. beautiful

2. show

3. prise

4. document

5. industrious

6. riot

7. hot

8. consolidate

9. palpable

10. assure

WORD 7, Usage

Correct the errors in word usage in the following sentences.

Example: The Pulitzer Prize is a honor.

Answer: The Pulitzer Prize is an honor.

1. I thought we could leave, but Joe ain't ready to go.

2. Nicholas loved music of all types, while Lou was very particular.

3. Although I set out twenty tomato plants this summer, none have any ripe fruit yet.

4. The show which is on Channel 42 at 10 tonight should be very interesting.

5. Jason should of arrived by now.

6. I like all winter sports accept curling, which I don't even understand.

7. The traffic was so light that we had no problem getting their on time.

8. No one RSVP'd, so I have no idea whose coming.

9. Although not nearly as dramatic as what was discussed in the popular press, the decreasing ozone levels have nonetheless been linked to climactic changes.

10. Each year the ocean currents cut further into the beach.

Chapter 8

PUNCTUATION

PUNCT 1a–c, The Comma 1

Correct the errors in the use of the comma in the following sentences.
For example: I limbered up for twenty minutes and I went for a five-mile run.

Correction: I limbered up for twenty minutes, and I went for a five-mile run.

1. He worked hard yet he was not feeling tired.

2. As Felix watched the cat ate her breakfast of Tuna Delight.

3. Last semester I had Professor Roop for history which has always been my favorite subject.

4. Yawning Mumia put down his book and went to bed.

5. My oldest brother Geoffrey usually comes for Thanksgiving.

6. Ben's favorite book, *The Lion, the Witch, and the Wardrobe*, was written by C. S. Lewis in 1950.

7. In summer, I get up very early.

8. Driving in the Indianapolis 500 which is one of America's premier races, was an immense thrill for Sharleen.

9. Taken together hot weather and no increase in electrical supply forebode even more widespread rolling blackouts.

10. Having gotten lost twice already Doug thought maybe it would be wise to ask for directions at the service station.

PUNCT 1d–g, The Comma 2

Correct the errors in the use of the comma in the following sentences.
For example: I need to go to the bookstore, the library and the registrar's.
Correction: I need to go to the bookstore, the library, and the registrar's.

1. The recipe specifically called for ripe, large, red tomatoes.

2. This fall Eliot was reading Thomas McGuane, Rick Bass and Alice Walker.

3. For this reason the committee voted to change the policy.

4. President Jimmy Carter may turn out to be more effective out of office than in unlike Lyndon Johnson.

5. Riding into a headwind, can help you improve your cycling endurance, power and technique.

6. John was elected by his peers to lead the team, and therefore feels both honored and pressured.

7. The cost of health care has increased for example at a rate that far outstrips inflation.

8. As the workweek has been shortened, productivity has increased not decreased.

9. Their new house on Willow Street is small square and energy efficient.

10. They will discover however that appeasement has historically achieved not resolution, but mere postponement.

PUNCT 1h–l, The Comma 3

Correct the errors in use of the comma in the following sentences.
For example: The enthusiastic audience called out "More! More!"
Correction: The enthusiastic audience called out, "More! More!"

1. I smiled and said "Yes I'll be there."

2. If you want to call Jessye has a phone.

3. Our reservations are for Friday October 26 through Sunday November 11.

4. Luke called yesterday and said "Congratulations on your new baby."

5. Lonnie gave me a ride from Tulsa Oklahoma to Paris Texas.

6. After the dinner check your answering machine for messages.

7. John is drinking water and Mary soda.

8. "Well please come in" said my father graciously.

9. The senator's aide said their office had received more than 1400 letters in favor of the bill.

10. Let's go now that we're ready.

PUNCT 1m, The Comma 4

Correct the following sentences by removing unnecessary commas.
For example: Maybe, you'll receive the letter today.
Correction: Maybe you'll receive the letter today.

1. Adela and her brother, watched *West Wing,* every week.

2. I drove, last week, to Pullman, Washington, to visit my best friends.

3. The critics panned the play, *Welcome Home,* as slow and pretentious.

4. If I, were you, I would leave before rush hour.

5. The small, gold, locket was a family heirloom.

6. He shipped me a box, that contained four hundred yo-yo's, missing strings.

7. He liked music by groups such as, A Tribe Called Quest, Massive Attack, and The Brand New Heavies.

8. Jobs, jobs, and jobs, was the theme of his campaign.

9. He came early, and left late, much to my surprise.

10. She loved to go to the museum, on Saturday, but he, preferred Sunday.

PUNCT 2, The Semicolon

Correct the following sentences by either adding or removing semicolons as appropriate. Some sentences may be correct as given.

For example: It was a cool, gray day, the beach was empty.

Correction: It was a cool, gray day; the beach was empty.

1. The drive from Akron to Cincinnati was long; but I didn't mind; nor did my sister.

2. The rapid decrease in computer hardware prices has put pressure on software developers to do the same, nonetheless, they have resisted the trend for the most part.

3. On one recent weekend I saw *Pearl Harbor*, which used extensive computer-generated simulations of an historical event, *The Matrix*, which explored virtual worlds accessed via mind control, and *Until the End of the World*, which presented computer-driven dream exploration—technology is both a major theme and tool of the film studios.

4. I was shocked when I drove the $20,000 car, it rode only a bit better than my current car, which has a book value of only $1,500.

5. Although I support universal access to health care; I disagree with coupling it to flat rating; providing access shouldn't eliminate underwriting entirely.

6. He was my best friend; and because of this he was always welcome in my family's home.

7. My family took a raft trip down the Colorado River, including the Horn Creek Rapids; which is rated 9 of a possible 10 in terms of difficulty of passage without capsizing, sinking, or otherwise being upset.

8. We thought we'd visit John on the way; but we ran out of time and had to pass by without stopping.

9. My sister's letter from Chobe National Park in Botswana took fourteen weeks to reach me; the letter and the park she described were both full of wonders.

10. The rainfall for the month of August was only four inches, however that was normal for the region.

PUNCT 3, The Colon

Correct the following sentences by either adding or removing colons as appropriate. Some sentences may be correct as given.

For example: Alastair counted up his Halloween catch; 38 candy bars, 7 different types of chewing gum, and miscellaneous fruit that he did not even bother to count.

Correction: Alastair counted up his Halloween catch: 38 candy bars, 7 different types of chewing gum, and miscellaneous fruit that he did not even bother to count.

1. I have passed along to my children one of my father's sayings, "When you borrow something, try to return it in better condition than you received it."

2. Scientists, in an effort to isolate what it is in food that makes most people evaluate it as "tasting good or delicious," have determined the single most important ingredient: fat.

3. On your way home please pick up a pound of cold cuts, a head of lettuce, and a video.

4. Today is a very good day for haying: plenty of sunshine, a light breeze, and low humidity.

5. We took the following route: Route 80 to Rock Springs, Route 187 to Farson, and Route 28 to South Pass City.

6. He speaks four languages, English, French, German, and Spanish.

7. Many vegetarians have a curious blind spot; They don't seem to realize that plants are just as alive as animals.

8. Professor Thomason argued that there was one reason the United States had not acted more decisively in Bosnia, it has no oil.

9. My aunt is fond of quoting from the Bible and regularly recites Luke 1: 2.

10. The Great Lakes include: Huron, Ontario, Michigan, Erie, and Superior.

PUNCT 4, The Apostrophe

Correct the following sentences by either adding or removing apostrophes as appropriate.

For example: Do you know the origin of the expression "Mind your *ps* and *qs*"?

Correction: Do you know the origin of the expression "Mind your p's and q's"?

1. Did you see the film *My Mothers Castle?*

2. My grandmother told me that the 38 hurricane was much worse than this years storm.

3. A snake sheds it's skin when its growing.

4. What is our companys policy regarding maternity leave?

5. I thought it was her's, but perhaps its really Bills.

6. I really enjoyed E. L. Doctorows novel *World's Fair*.

7. Oy! Jon's and Emily's dog, Bumper, has knocked over our garbage again. Now I know why thats his' name.

8. He accepted the Chief's of Staff recommendation.

9. Until this semester I had never used Petersens's Theory.

10. The teachers union and our school board seemed forever in negotiation.

PUNCT 5, Quotation Marks

Correct the following sentences by either adding, altering, or removing quotation marks and related punctuation as appropriate.

For example: O. Henry's short story The Gift of the Magi was included in his first book of stories, "The Four Million."

Correction: O. Henry's short story "The Gift of the Magi" was included in his first book of stories, The Four Million.

1. "Where you place your commas is one of my teacher's "things", so I always double check my work", said Elaine.

2. "Would you like to come to dinner with us"? Mary asked.

3. When I read computer magazines I find all the technobabble confusing: "RAM," "ROM" and "bytes"—who dreams up these terms?

4. Milan told me that "Faulkner wrote the novel 'As I Lay Dying' in only six weeks."

5.   "I hope you'll come to our party tonight, said Alison.

   "Me too, I replied. "but I have to work until 11."

   "That's no problem; she said. It doesn't even start until 10, and I doubt you'll miss anything. Just come as you are after work.

6. Last year when I reread *The Declaration of Independence*, I discovered it was much more interesting than I ever remembered it to be.

7. Ryan's research paper for English 101, The Changing Status of Euthanasia in the United States, helped him clinch an "A" in the course.

8. Lawrence had mixed feelings about hearing the president quoting from the Eagles' song Take It to the Limit—was this the movie "The Big Chill" come to life?

9. The proceeds go to a worthy cause, the "Jaime. L. Barzenté Memorial Fund."

10. "Where's the power switch,"? said Tom, as smoke poured from his computer.

PUNCT 6a, The Period

Correct the errors in the use of the period in the following sentences.

For example: Dorothy asked me if was I aware that sit-ups could strain my back?

Correction: Dorothy asked me if was I aware that sit-ups could strain my back.

1. If you know the Latin meaning abbreviated by am and pm, you will find it easier to remember which one to use.

2. One of the experimental drugs being used to combat AIDS is A.Z.T.

3. I wondered if he knew what the U.S.D.A. stamp on the meat stood for.

4. One of the most woeful scenes in all of Shakespeare is in *King Lear* V, iii.

5. Tintin's best friend is Capt Horatio Haddock.

6. Last December he was promoted to President at Kahrdif, Inc..

7. Has your teacher ever told you to avoid using *etc* in your writing?

8. When Bert graduates from medical school next month he will be Dr Umberto Baldi.

9. They live just off South Main St, I think.

10. Junko asked me what time I had arrived at work this morning?

PUNCT 6b–c, The Question Mark and Exclamation Point

Correct the errors in the use of the question mark and exclamation point in the following sentences.

For example: When is he coming.

Correction: When is he coming?

1. Joyce said, "Do you know whether bus or subway is the better way to get to Avenue J from here."

2. As usual for this region, the weather was sunny!

3. Which route to Des Moines has less traffic, John wanted to know?

4. "Can I come too," my sister asked.

5. Louis asked me which class I liked best?

6. Rolf asked me, "What is the difference between a CD and CD-ROM."

7. Wow. This pie is fabulous.

8. Whose book is that.

9. "Is that your book," Lisa asked me?

10. I could not remember when they were coming?

PUNCT 6d–h, Other Punctuation

Correct the punctuation errors involving the use of the dash, period, question mark, exclamation point, parentheses, brackets, ellipses, and the slash in the following sentences.

For example: Batman and Robin; also known as the "dynamic duo"; have been popular with three generations.

Correction: Batman and Robin—also known as the "dynamic duo"—have been popular with three generations.

1. One awkward, but acceptable, solution to the problem of sexism in pronouns is the use of *him, her* as well as *he or she.*

2. When in Rome (as the saying goes) do as the Romans do.

3. The senator said, "The president's position (on Senate Resolution 553) is encouraging and will help him pass his own agenda later in the session."

4. "Our class meets in that new science building. What's its name? Something Hall . . . . Burstein . . . . Gurstein? I can't remember," said John.

5. I still remember the opening lines to Shakespeare's Sonnet LXXIII:

   "That time of year thou mayst in me behold

   When yellow leaves, or none, or few, do hang

   Upon those boughs which shake against the cold."

6. Leave now? We just got here—

7. The Red's starting pitcher, my neighbor's son, Jason, wound up and delivered an 80 mph fastball.

8. I was happy I had voted for him, until he actually won the election.

9. The lecture, a ninety-minute torrent of anecdotes, facts, figures, and numerous slides, left me exhilarated but exhausted.

10. John switched his horses to compressed alfalfa from locally grown hay. Too often it caused colic.

Chapter 9

MECHANICS

MECH 1a–d, Capitals 1

Correct the errors in capitalization in the following sentences.
For example: Last Fall we hiked in the wind river range.
Correction: Last fall we hiked in the Wind River Range.

1. Unfortunately, stargazers living this far North can't see the southern cross.

2. When James "joe" Jackson sang last week at the 3rd avenue grill, the crowd roared its approval.

3. The Cold War may be over, but we're still paying the bill.

4. The baptist church in my town sponsors a Community food shelf.

5. In the last four months the missouri and mississippi rivers reached record flood levels, but the hudson river was below normal.

6. I sat late into the night with my family to see Neil Armstrong walk on the moon on july 20, 1969, during the *apollo 11* mission.

7. Last quarter the Ford and Chrysler Companies reported increased sales, while at General Motors Corporation sales were flat.

8. My cousin Lou-Lou is the Founder of cara, the committee against ridiculous acronyms.

9. Once labor day weekend rolls around, you know that Summer is really over.

10. My Mother is a protestant, and my Father, a muslim.

MECH 1e–j, Capitals 2

Correct the errors in capitalization in the following sentences.

For example: When the storm came through, the weather turned cold.
no, it became bitter.

Correction: When the storm came through, the weather turned cold. No, it became bitter.

1. In a recent article, commentator Julia Webb wrote, "for the first time in U.S. history, by the year 2002, more than fifty percent of all American jobs will require at least one year of college."

2. I read the *daily plains record* every day to keep up on local news.

3. During the Spring Semester Dmitri is going to enroll in Calculus, History, and English.

4. I think she bought one of the new Apple Notebook Computers.

5. Who reports on the News Media? the News Media do.

6. Have you read Tom Wolfe's *the bonfire of the vanities*?

7. Our city has two Mosques, four Temples, and twenty-eight Churches of various denominations.

8. Ford Trucks outsell all other makes in new england.

9. During my first Semester at the university of Arizona, I was swamped with work, but very happy.

10. In what year did Fitzgerald write *the great gatsby*?

MECH 2, Abbreviations

Correct the errors in the use of abbreviations in the following sentences. For example: Laura's commission on new sales was 8 pct.
Correction: Laura's commission on new sales was 8 percent.

1. He reported to Sgt. Bilko.

2. The president announced that the new policy was designed to protect our natl. security.

3. Aristotle was born in B.C. 384.

4. Dr. C. Everett Koop, M.D. gave the keynote address.

5. For the trip they packed clothes, food, games, etc.

6. The dissolution of the Soviet Union has generated much debate over the future of N.A.T.O.

7. If we leave now, we'll get home in the p.m.

8. When people claim that electric cars are pollution-free, i.e., emit no pollutants, they forget one important fact: the power plant that generated the electricity used by the car isn't pollution-free.

9. Do you know the topic of Prof. Montrose's lecture for our 9 am seminar?

10. British & American English differ in many small ways; e.g., we place a period after the abbreviation for *Mister* (Mr.), whereas the British do not.

MECH 3, Numbers

Correct the errors in use of numbers in the following sentences.
For example: Devon was born in nineteen seventy-one.
Correction: Devon was born in 1971.

1. Armand cut the plank into four six-foot sections.

2. Charles Lindbergh began his historic 2-day flight on May 20th,
   1927 from Roosevelt Field, Long Island.

3. Skosh thought the boat out to Catalina Island was more than
   $20.00.

4. American Airlines currently has over six hundred twenty planes.

5. Over the holidays we saw four films, two plays, and 13 videos.

6. The competition was very close: only 1/8 of a second separated
   the 6 sprinters.

7. At the beginning of the 20th century, individuals traveled largely
   by horse; now we drive cars. What will we be doing at the end of
   the 21st century?

8. The final score was Tigers eight, Panthers two.

9. Our state budget is over 2,300,000,000 dollars.

10. We got up at seven a.m. and swam before breakfast.

MECH 4, Italics/Underlining

Correct the following sentences by adding or removing italics as appropriate. Remember to indicate italics with continuous underlining (such as this sample).

For example: John told me to check The Cambridge Encyclopedia of Language.

Correction: John told me to check <u>The Cambridge Encyclopedia of Language</u>.

1. Linda likes Microsoft Word, but I prefer Claris MacWrite.

2. The most commonly occurring word in English is the.

3. I asked him to explain what noblesse oblige means.

4. Did you read last week's cover story in Newsweek?

5. Tina objected to Dickens's overfrequent use of a deus ex machina to resolve his fantastically-plotted novels.

6. Prabhu rode the Amtrak Empire Builder from Chicago, Illinois, to Portland, Oregon.

7. James Fenimore Cooper's The Last of the Mohicans was made into a movie 166 years after its original publication as the second of *The Leather–Stocking Tales.*

8. The radio show All Things Considered is considered liberal by conservatives and conservative by liberals; maybe that is how the producers came to name the show.

9. His class is reading Dante's Divine Comedy in parallel texts.

10. Unable to travel, she was awarded the Nobel Prize *in absentia.*

MECH 5, The Hyphen

Correct the following sentences by either adding or removing hyphens as appropriate.

For example: His one year old car still looked brand-new.

Correction: His one-year-old car still looked brand new.

1. I am very close to my brother in law.

2. The ex Metropolitan Opera soprano joined our community chorus and improved the entire section's performance.

3. Are you looking forward to the beginning of the school-year?

4. Our class voted twenty one to seventeen for more study time.

5. In pre revolutionary America the colonists were subjects of the king of England.

6. The police officer told me that J walking was illegal in this town.

7. The groom nearly fainted when the best-man couldn't find the wedding ring.

8. The governor elect will face many difficult issues this year.

9. When I was a thirteen year old, I played a lot of base-ball.

10. From the eighteenth- to the twentieth-century, the West evolved from a pre industrial society to a post industrial one.

MECH 6a, Basic Spelling Rules

Correct the spelling errors in the following sentences by applying the basic spelling rules.

For example: I beleive that he'll be over by eight o'clock.

Correction: I believe that he'll be over by eight o'clock.

1. I'm hopeing we can see Jeri before she leaves.

2. Professor Guimard is very knowledgable about plate tectonics.

3. Lofti Zadeh was lying down thinking when an idea suddenly occured to him; half an hour later he had laid out all the funda-mentals of the feild now known as Fuzzy Logic.

4. How much did you say you payed for those peachs?

5. I sent the package via Express, so he ought to recieve it by noon tomorrow.

6. No sooner had the city finished paveing our street than the Water Department tore it back up again.

7. I love my brother, but I still think he's wierd.

8. These days, most people don't bother to pick up pennys.

9. It might sound odd, but our paper has two editor-in-chiefs.

10. We spend a lot of time with our nieghbors.

MECH 6a, Words that Sound Alike

The following sentences contain homophones used in error. Replace the incorrect word in each sentence with its correct sound-alike.

For example: After much deliberation, he decided to except their job offer.

Correction: After much deliberation, he decided to accept their job offer.

1. In our library, cereal acquisitions is on the 3rd floor.

2. In the 100-meter finals, Sarah was third and I was forth.

3. My father is sight manager for the new Deeter Building construction project.

4. My teacher recommended that we always read the forward, as it usually defines the scope and approach of the book that follows.

5. All the people I know with personal stationary are of my parents' generation.

6. When the passed president of the AFL–CIO addressed our school, he complemented the White House's new labor relations policy.

7. If their coming with us, they have too hurry up.

8. I would rather work now, finish the reading, and than go to the late show.

9. Whose playing against the Utah Jazz tonight?

10. The teenage years can be a period of extreme pier pressure.

Chapter 10

DESIGN

DESIGN 2a–c, Basic Computer Formatting

A mock-up of a student essay is shown on the next page, and questions regarding this mock-up follow it.

Within the mock-up, lettered line segments mark a number of elements. For each such marked element, provide the appropriate margin or spacing. The first one is done for you as an example.

In addition, there are five formatting flaws in this mock-up. Using the spaces provided, list each formatting error and describe what should have been done instead.

(b)

(a)

Smith 1

Lorem ipsum dolor sit amet, consectetuer adipiscing elit, sed diam nonummy nibh euismod tincidunt ut laoreet

(f) dolore magna aliquam erat volutpat. Ut wisi enim ad minim veniam, quis nostrud exerci tation ullamcorper suscipit lobortis nisl ut aliquip ex ea commodo consequat.

MAJOR HEADING

Duis autem vel eum iriure dolor in hendrerit in vulputate velit esse molestie consequat, abitando

(c) quest'anno in toscano. Vel illum dolore eu feugiat nulla **(e)** facilisis at vero eros et accumsan et iusto odio dignissim qui blandit.

Subheading

Praesent luptatum ril delenit augue duis dolore te feugait nulla facilisi. Lorem ipsum dolor sit amet, consectetuer adipiscing elit, sed diam nonummy nibh euismod tincidunt:

- laoreet dolore magna aliquam erat volutpat
- enim ad minim veniam nostrud
- exerci tation ullam corper suscipit
- lobortis nisl ut aliquip ex ea commodo consequat.

Duis autem vel eum iriure dolor in hendrerit in vulputate velit essere molestie consequat, vel illum dolore eu feugiat nulla facilisis et tierne nog. Duis autem vel eum iriure dolor in hendrerit in vulputate velit esse molestie consequat, vel illum dolore eu feugiat nulla facilisis et tierne nog.

(d)

   (a) <u>top of page</u> to <u>last name/page number</u>: 1/2 inch

1. **(b)** top margin:

2. **(c)** left margin:

3. **(d)** bottom margin:

4. **(e)** right margin:

5. **(f)** linespacing:

   Formatting Errors:

6. _____

7. _____

8. _____

9. _____

10. _____

Chapter 11

WRITING AN ARGUMENT / WRITING ABOUT LITERATURE

ARGUE 1b, Facts versus Claims

For each of the following statements identify them as either a fact or a claim. If the statement is a fact, rewrite it, inventing as necessary, to make the statement into a claim. If the statement is already a claim, simply label it as such. For example, given:

(   )   The FCC has scheduled HDTV broadcasting to begin in all major metropolitan areas of the U.S. by 2002.

First identify the statement as given as a "fact." Then, freely inventing the information you need to make the conversion, rewrite the sentence and convert it into a "claim." Thus, the completed answer might look like this:

(fact   )   The FCC has scheduled HDTV broadcasting to begin in all major metropolitan areas of the U.S. by 2002.

(claim   )   By 2002 HDTV will revolutionize television broadcasting in all major metropolitan areas of the U.S.

1. (   ) Euthanasia is a right that every American should have the option of electing.

   (   )

2. (   ) Some animal rights advocates object to the use of animals for medical research and testing.

   (   )

3. (   ) The use of grades in schools stifles creativity.

   (   )

4. (   ) Snowboarding became an Olympic medal sport
   in 1998.

   (   )

5. (   ) U.S. immigration policy still reflects cold war
   biases.

   (   )

6. (   ) *Titanic* was the most expensive movie ever made.

   (   )

7. (   ) Global warming has created the conditions responsible for El Niño.

   (   )

8. (   ) U.S. DOT studies have revealed that in collisions
   between cars and trucks/sport utility vehicles, 80% of the fatalities
   occur in the cars.

   (   )

9. (   ) World hunger is a problem that will never
   be solved.

   (   )

10. (   ) Though 30% of all cancers are associated with
    tobacco use, the government has not made it an illegal substance.

    (   )

ARGUE 2a, Syllogisms

For each of the following syllogisms (major premise, minor premise, and conclusion), state whether they are "valid" or "fallacious." If fallacious, state why the conclusion is not valid. For example, given:

a.   On average, males tend to score higher on the SAT Math exam than females. (*major premise*)

b.   SAT Math scores accurately reflect math ability. (*minor premise*)

c.   Therefore, on average, males have higher math abilities than females. (*conclusion*)

FALLACIOUS. The conclusion is invalid because it assumes that the minor

premise is a fact, when it is arguably an assertion. Some research has con-

cluded that this test is gender-biased; that is, males tend to score higher

because of gender biases in the test, not because of greater ability.

1a.   All men with chalk dust on their hands are schoolteachers.
 b.   John has chalk dust on his hands.
 c.   Therefore, John is a schoolteacher.

2a.   Good nutrition is essential for good health.
 b.   Lynda eats well.
 c.   Therefore, Lynda is healthy.

3a. The rooster crows every morning shortly before dawn.
  b. The sun comes up every morning at dawn.
  c. Therefore, the rooster's crowing brings the sun.

_____

_____

_____

4a. All fish live in water.
  b. Lobster live in water.
  c. Therefore, lobster are fish.

_____

_____

_____

5a. Our solar system has only one star in it.
  b. The Sun is a star in our solar system.
  c. Therefore, the Sun is the only star in our solar system.

_____

_____

_____

6a. The Squirrel Nut Zippers have recorded two CDs.
  b. I have two CDs in my collection.
  c. Therefore, I have both Squirrel Nut Zippers CDs.

_____

_____

_____

7a. More and more people are getting their news via the Web.
 b. The readership of newspapers is declining.
 c. Therefore, the Web is responsible for declining newspaper readership.

_____

_____

_____

8a. All democrats are liberals.
 b. Will is a liberal.
 c. Therefore, Will is a democrat.

_____

_____

_____

9a. Asia is the most densely populated continent.
 b. Beijing is a densely populated city.
 c. Therefore, Beijing is in Asia.

_____

_____

_____

10a. The Metro often runs late when it rains hard.
 b. It is raining hard today.
 c. Therefore, the Metro will be late today.

_____

_____

_____

LIT 2, Conventions for Writing about Literature

The following brief piece about Ernest Hemingway's "The Snows of Kilimanjaro" contains a number of violations of the conventions and suggestions contained in **LIT 2**. Rewrite the piece making appropriate edits and be prepared to discuss and explain your edits. Use MLA formatting conventions (see **MLA DOCU 4** in the handbook).

The Age of Wisdom, The Age of Despair:

Hemingway on Safari

Ernest Hemingway's short story *The Snows of Kilimanjaro* was the unhappy story of a man, Harry, on safari with his wife, and dying of an infection resulting from a scratch from a thorn bush received some two weeks before the story opens. The action takes place over a period of two days, during which Harry drinks whiskey-and-soda, sleeps, dreams stories he wishes he had written, and argues with his wife. During the second night of the story, Harry dies while dreaming of flying past Mt. Kilimanjaro, Africa's highest peak at 19,710 feet.

The author opens the story by saying:

"The marvellous thing is that it's painless," he said. "That's how you know when it starts."

"Is it really?"

"Absolutely. I'm awfully sorry about the odor though. That must bother you."

"Don't! Please don't."

"Look at them," he said. "Now is it sight or is it scent that brings them like that?"

And so the essay is off and running, with the author dying and his wife, Helen, not at all sure if Hemingway is telling the truth or just keeping a stiff upper lip. Like much of Hemingway's short fiction, this novella, collected in "The First Forty-nine," published in 1938 by Scribners and Sons, highlights the tensions between life's inherent drama and the author's preoccupation with separating himself from that drama. Here Harry is dying and he refers to the whole event as pain-free, even as his body is being ravaged by spreading gangrene, and his conversations with his wife are marked by bitterness as he calls her names, all the while never even addressing her by name.

Thus a life-threatening situation, in which most of us would rely heavily upon family, instead finds Hemingway armoring himself with whiskey, distancing himself from his wife, and withdrawing into delusional isolation.

Though Ernest Hemingway was relatively young and famous at the time of writing this story, he comes across as world-weary and aged beyond his years. Hemingway said that his goal was to write the truth; sadly, here we find that the truth is a world of misery.

Chapter 12

SPECIAL KINDS OF WRITING

SPECIAL 1a, E-mail

A sample E-mail from a student to a professor appears below. The message contains ten violations of the guidelines in **SPECIAL 1a**. Name each of the errors in the spaces provided.

```
TC: arosa@lynx.uvm.edu

FROM: psmith@cat.uvm.edu

DATE/TIME: 24FEB02; 21:17:12

SUBJ:

Dear Prof. Rosa,

I just returned from a trip and wanted to check
on our current assignment b/c I lost my sylla-
bus. ;)  IS IT TRUE THAT OUR FIRST DRAFT IS DUE
MCNDAY? That's wut John P told me. But this is
nct enough tmie to get the paper off to a good
start. So, please let me know what's up ASAP.
TTFN,

Peter S.
```

1. _____

2. _____

_____

3. _____

4. _____

5. _____

6. _____

7. _____

8. _____

9. _____

10. _____

SPECIAL 2a, Formatting a Business Letter

A sample business letter by a student seeking employment appears on the following page. Lettered line segments mark a number of elements on the page. Complete the following list by indicating next to each letter the appropriate margin, position, or spacing. The first one is done for you as an example.

In addition, there are eight formatting flaws in this sample page; list them and describe what should have been done instead. Use the spaces provided.

    (a) <u>top of page</u> to <u>top of return address</u>: 6-12 linespaces (use this variation to balance the letter visually on the page from top to bottom)

1.   **(b)** linespacing:

2.   **(c)** left margin:

3.   **(d)** bottom margin:

4.   **(e)** right margin:

5.   appropriate letter type (full block; modified block; indented)?

6. _____

7. _____

8. _____

9. _____

10. _____

11. _____

12. _____

13. _____

(a)

207 Coolidge Hall
University of Vermont
Burlington, Vermont 05401

(b)

February 1, 1998
Mr. Harold Von Braun
Director, Management Training Center
Acme Pyrotechnics, Inc.
Tuscon, AZ   87654

Dear Mr. Von Braun,   **(e)**

(c)   Lorem ipsum dolor sit amet, consectetuer adipiscing
elit, sed diam nonummy.   Nibh euismod tincidunt ut
laoreet dolore magna aliquam erat volutpat.
Duis autem vel eum iriure dolor in hendrerit in vulputate
velit esse molestie consequat, abitando quest'anno in
toscana. Vel illum dolore eu feugiat nulla facilisis
at vero eros et accumsan et iusto odio dignissim qui
blandit.
Ut wisi enim ad minim veniam, quis nostrud exerci tation
ullamcorper suscipit lobortis nisl ut aliquip ex ea
commodo consequat. Duis autem vel eum iriure dolor in
hendrerit in vulputate.
Velit esse molestie consequat, vel illum dolore eu
feugiat nulla facilisis at vero eros et accumsan et iusto
odio dignissim qui blandit praesent luptatum.
Ut wisi enim ad minim veniam.
Sincerely Yours
William C. Aiote
William C. Aiote

Encl. Resume

(d)

Chapter 13

THE RESEARCH PAPER

RESCH 1, Conducting Library and Internet Research

Complete the crossword puzzle which begins on the next page.
All the answers correspond to various resources, including the Internet,
generally available in the library to assist you in conducting research.

Down

2. Number used to locate books within the stacks.
3. Acronym for Compact Disc, Read-Only Memory.
4. Good source of geographical information, especially maps.
5. Internet discussion group implemented as subscription-only e-mail.
7. General term for magazines, journals, and newspapers.
8. Name of the world-wide network of computers sharing information on almost every conceivable subject.
9. Abbreviation most often used when referring to the World Wide Web.
10. Opposite of online.
11. One of these typically contains information that is updated every year.
13. One of the best-known Internet search engines.
16. Term for a summary of an article or book.
18. One of the ways in which card catalog information is organized.
19. A search by _____ in an electronic card catalog can greatly increase the scope and possibilities of your search.

Across

1. Generally an excellent first resource for a topic new to you.
6. Acronym for an Internet site's address.
9. Source of brief biographical sketches on contemporary Americans.
12. Author of a very useful guide to the reference books.
14. Best-known guide to popular periodical literature.
15. Term meaning any store of information, typically large and accessed by computer.
20. Principal tool for finding books within the library; now often an online resource.
21. Listing of books, articles, and other materials on a particular topic; often located at the end of an article or book.
22. One of the ways in which card catalog information is organized.
23. Internet discussion group open to all for reading and posting messages.
24. Type of software used to access Web sites; Netscape Navigator and Internet Explorer are two of the most widely used of these.

RESCH 5b, Avoiding Plagiarism

For each of the quotations provided write an acceptable paraphrase, that is, one that avoids plagiarism. Pay particular attention to the word choice and sentence structure of the original.

1. "America is a throw-away society that discards every year 41 million tons of food and yard waste, 13 million tons of metal, 12 million tons of glass, and 10 million tons of plastic." (after Jim Hightower's *War on Waste*)

_____

_____

_____

_____

_____

2. "All light sources emit waves uniformly in all directions. The amplitude of the waves is perceived by the eye as brightness, or luminance. In space the light waves from stars travel unimpeded and their self-propagating quality perpetuates them infinitely." (after Jeff Burger's *Desktop Multimedia Bible*)

_____

_____

_____

_____

_____

_____

3. "The sperm whale is the largest of the toothed whales. Moby Dick was a sperm whale. Generally, male toothed whales are larger than the females. Female sperm whales may grow 35 to 40 feet in length, while the males may reach 60 feet." (after Richard Hendrick et al.'s *The Voyage of the Mimi*)

_____

_____

_____

_____

_____

4. "The humble Teddy Bear not only launched an industry and increased Teddy Roosevelt's popularity, it also fostered the American tendency to focus on the personality rather than the policies of our political leaders." (after Brier, Rosenzweig, and Brown's *Who Built America?*)

_____

_____

_____

_____

_____

_____

_____

5. "On first inspection, the novels of Hemingway and Fitzgerald seem altogether at odds: Hemingway's abrupt dialog and action-filled story lines have a swagger to them that is a world apart from Fitzgerald's polished conversations and drawing room drama. But beyond these superficial differences, both authors create characters aching to find meaning in the confusing modernity of the early twentieth century." (after Oscar Deep's *Defining the Modern Mind*)

_____

_____

_____

_____

_____

_____

_____

6. "Astronauts from over twenty nations have gone into space and they all come back, amazingly enough, saying the very same thing: the earth is a small, blue place of profound beauty that we must take care of. For each, the journey into space, whatever its original intents and purposes, became above all a spiritual one." (after Al Reinhert's *For All Mankind*)

_____

_____

_____

_____

7. "What is technophobia really about? It's not an unhealthy and unjustified fear of confusing machinery that may break, bringing potential embarrassment or worse. No, it's a natural reaction to poorly designed machines." (after Donald Norman's *Defending Human Attributes in the Age of the Machine*)

8. "One of the usual things about education in mathematics in the United States is its relatively impoverished vocabulary. Whereas the student completing elementary school will already have a vocabulary for most disciplines of many hundreds, even thousands of words, the typical student will have a mathematics vocabulary of only a couple of dozen words." (after Marvin Minsky's *The Society of Mind*)

9. "Underlying all great works of art is the artist's completely private and unfathomable tenacity—his or her unrelenting pursuit of an idea, a feeling, or a vision beyond the boundaries where most of us would stop. Travelling into places beyond our ken, they return with artifacts that we can inspect in the safety of a gallery or mu-

seum. But just as we don't mistake a trip to the natural history museum for a visit to the jungle itself, nor should we mistake a visit to an art museum for the creative ferment of the artist's studio. The gilt-framed museum painting, hung in front of speechless crowds shuffling respectfully past, is no more alive than the stuffed museum lion, posed with its false glass eyes mocking menace and forever unmoving. And if we turn to ask the artists themselves about these pieces? They are nowhere to be seen, for they are packed and already gone." (after Thomas Murphy's essay, "Private Experience and Public Display" in *The Collected Works of T. D. Murphy*)

_____

_____

_____

_____

_____

_____

_____

_____

_____

_____

10. "In archetypal symbolism, clothing represents *persona*, the first view the public gains of us. Persona is a kind of camouflage which lets others know only what we wish them to know about us, and nothing more. But the persona is not just a mask to hide behind, it is also a presence which eclipses the mundane personality. In this sense, persona or mask is an outward signal of rank, virtue, character, and authority." (after Clarissa Pinkola Estés's *Women Who Run with the Wolves*)

_____

_____

_____

_____

_____

_____

_____

_____

RESCH 6, Integrating Borrowed Material

Quotations are generally used to support and develop an idea already presented in your paper. For this exercise first read the quotation provided and then develop a claim that can be supported and developed by the quotation. Second, briefly state your claim; and third, write a paragraph that employs all, or some, of the quotation provided to support and develop your claim.

Be sure to use a clear signal phrase (for example, using author name, authority, and selecting a precise and appropriate introductory verb—such as "supports," "explains," "argues," etc.). Such signal phrases (1) help integrate the quotation smoothly into your own line of argument, (2) help your reader understand for what purpose the quotation is being used, and (3) help your reader distinguish your own thoughts from those of your quoted source.

For example:

Quotation and source: "The size of the 'hole' in the ozone layer would amaze most citizens." Peter Cannis, Director, Center for Atmospheric Study, in *The 1998 Annual Review of the Environment*, p 47.

Claim:

The ozone problem is serious and merits our attention.

Paragraph incorporating quotation:

The steady diminution of the ozone layer has caused the appearance of a vast area of thinning most often referred to as a "hole." Many scientists are concerned that the general populace is too little concerned and informed about the problem. Dr. Peter Cannis, Director of the Center for Atmospheric Study warned, "The size of the hole in the ozone layer would amaze most citizens" (47). It is, in fact, the size of North America.

1. Quotation and source: "The Information Superhighway will provide a general intellectual mobility for the American people that our national system of interstate highways has heretofore provided for transportation." Iam C. Piu, Founder, Americans for the 21st Century. Address to the National Press Club, 12 Jan 2001: "The Next Twenty Years in U.S. Information Technology."

Claim:

_____

_____

Paragraph incorporating quotation:

_____

_____

_____

_____

_____

_____

_____

_____

_____

_____

_____

_____

_____

_____

_____

_____

_____

2. Quotation and source: "Though to our eyes in the early twenty-first century Henry David Thoreau lived in an America that seems wild, unspoiled and largely undeveloped, to Thoreau this same world was one already in physical and moral decline, seemingly being devoured before his very eyes." Benjamin Austin, in *Perspective in American Life and Literature*, page 38.

Claim:

_____

_____

Paragraph incorporating quotation:

_____

_____

_____

_____

_____

_____

_____

_____

_____

_____

_____

_____

_____

_____

_____

_____

_____

3. Quotation and source: "It doesn't matter where you live. Long distances used to be a moat that both insulated and isolated people from workers on the other side of the world. But every day, technology narrows that moat inch by inch. Every person in the world is on the verge of becoming both a coworker and a competitor to every one of us.... Technological change is going to reach out and sooner or later change something fundamental in your ... world." Andrew S. Grove, President and CEO, Intel Corporation, in *Only the Paranoid Survive*, 1997, p 5.

Claim:

_____

_____

Paragraph incorporating quotation:

_____

_____

_____

_____

_____

_____

_____

_____

_____

_____

_____

_____

_____

_____

_____

Chapter 14

MLA DOCUMENTATION
AND FORMAT

MLA DOCU 1, MLA In-Text Citations

For each of the following exercises write a passage incorporating the quoted material and giving an MLA-style in-text citation. Use signal phrases as indicated.

For example:

Format: Quote the following author using a signal phrase.

Author: Giuliano Procacci

Quote: "Yet it was not until 1930 that, for the first time in the history of Italy, the value of industrial production overtook that of agriculture."

Source: *History of the Italian People*, p. 379

Context: This is the only document by this author being used.

Possible Answer:

Of the slow-coming industrialization of Italy, Procacci notes that "it was not until 1930 that, for the first time in the history of Italy, the value of industrial production overtook that of agriculture" (379).

1. Format: Quote the following author without using a signal phrase.

   Author: Richard Adams

   Quote: "Human beings say, 'It never rains but it pours.' This is not very apt, for it frequently does rain without pouring. The rabbits' proverb is better expressed. They say, 'One cloud feels lonely.'"

   Source: *Watership Down*, fiction, chapter 23, p. 184

   Context: This is the only document by this author being used.

2. Format: Quote the following author using a signal phrase.

   Author: Richard Adams

   Quote: "Human beings say, 'It never rains but it pours.' This is
              not very apt, for it frequently does rain without pour-
              ing. The rabbits' proverb is better expressed. They say,
              'One cloud feels lonely.'"

   Source: *Watership Down*, fiction, chapter 23, p. 184

   Context: This is one of two documents by this author being
              used.

   _____

   _____

   _____

   _____

3. Format: Quote the following authors without using a signal
              phrase.

   Authors: Charles Heimler and Charles Neal

   Quote: "A cloud is a collection of water droplets or ice crystals
              in the air. It is formed when water vapor is cooled and
              changed into water droplets or ice crystals."

   Source: *Principles of Science*, p. 234

   Context: This is the only document by these authors being used.

   _____

   _____

   _____

   _____

4. Format: Quote the following authors using a signal phrase.

Author(s): Charles Heimler and Charles Neal

Quote: "A cloud is a collection of water droplets or ice crystals in the air. It is formed when water vapor is cooled and changed into water droplets or ice crystals."

Source: *Principles of Science*, p. 234

Context: This is one of three documents by these authors being used.

———————————————————————

———————————————————————

———————————————————————

———————————————————————

5. Format: Quote the following author using a signal phrase.

Author: Reginald J. Symington

Quote: "NATO's muddled expansion is so fraught with competing strategies that it has simultaneously threatened Moscow and made overtures to Russia to join the alliance itself."

Source: "NATO at the Crossroads," in *Foreign Affairs*, April 1996, p. 267

Context: This is one of two articles by this author being used.

———————————————————————

———————————————————————

———————————————————————

———————————————————————

6. Format: Quote the following author using a signal phrase.
   Author: Allen Ginsberg
   Quote: "I saw the best minds of my generation destroyed by madness / starving hysterical naked."
   Source: "HOWL Parts I and Part II," poem, lines 1-2
   Context: This is the only piece by this author being used.

_____

_____

_____

_____

7. Format: Quote the following author using a signal phrase.
   Author: Anne Tierney
   Quote: "Computers have only very recently become common outside narrowly defined locations such as academia, business, and the military. We are just beginning to understand what the age of 'personal computing' will mean to our culture."
   Source: Personal Interview, 22 July 2001
   Context: This is the only document by this author being used.

_____

_____

_____

_____

8. Format: Quote the following authors without using a signal
              phrase.

   Authors: Elizabeth McMahan, Susan Day, and Robert Funk
   Quote: "Rhythm can affect us powerfully. We respond almost
              automatically to the beat of a drum, the thumping of
              our heart, the pulsing of an engine. Poetic rhythm,
              usually more subtle, is made by repeating stresses and
              pauses."
   Source: *Literature and the Writing Process*, pp. 411-12
   Context: This is the only document by these authors being used.

   _____

   _____

   _____

   _____

9. Format: Quote the following authors using a signal phrase.
   Authors: Elizabeth McMahan, Susan Day, and Robert Funk
   Quote: "Rhythm can affect us powerfully. We respond almost
              automatically to the beat of a drum, the thumping of
              our heart, the pulsing of an engine. Poetic rhythm,
              usually more subtle, is made by repeating stresses and
              pauses."
   Source: *Literature and the Writing Process*, pp. 411-12
   Context: This is one of three documents by these authors being used.

   _____

   _____

   _____

   _____

10. Format: Quote the following author using a signal phrase.

     Authors: Corporate Author, Solar United Now (SUN)

     Quote: "Solar power is rapidly becoming financially viable primarily due to increasing solar conversion efficiencies and improved manufacturing. It would in fact compete favorably now with coal and oil if it were not for those industries' 'subsidies' in the form of federal policies, laws, and tax code provisions."

     Source: *A Solar Primer*, p. 44

     Context: This is the only document by this author being used.

_____

_____

_____

_____

_____

_____

_____

_____

MLA DOCU 2, MLA List of Works Cited—Electronic Sources

This exercise is based on the research process of a student preparing a paper that must follow MLA conventions. You are supplied with student D. Smith's *unformatted* notes on these electronic sources (see next page). Using these notes, prepare a set of sorted, correct bibliography cards.

This exercise will help you review the MLA conventions; it also points out a time-saving lesson: look at the format you must use *before* you create your notes so that you can collect the necessary information and then write your notes in the correct format right from the start.

For example, given the following note:

```
Fred Hampton via e-mail
subject line: "North Dakota Arts Council Policy"
date: June 29th, 01
Fred said this is a "near-final" draft;
final to be published in August
```

you would create this MLA-style bibliography card:

Hampton, Fred. "North Dakota Arts Council

Policy." E-mail to D. Smith.

29 June 2001.

Doug Reilly's essay Mark Twain and American Politics
found at UBoston American Authors Forum; creation
date:11JAN98   URL was www.uboston.edu/authors/clemens-
twain/   my access date: June 13, 2001
good review article of Twain's activities; use this one.
===========================
Sarah Lawrence, <u>Mark Twain</u>, a chapter in her book Manifest Destiny and American Frontier Literature. found at
UNebraska's gopher site. Publication date:20OCT96
URL unebraska.edu/AmerLit/essays/SLawrence/
manifest_destiny.doc
found on June 22, 2001   helpful bibliography
===========================
Robert Manzini's book Plains States Imagination. 1995.
ftp'd from ftp: seemu/litcritonline/manzini/psi.doc
picked up 18 June 2001
===========================
email letter from Professor Alice Benton Smith; subject
line: role of Clemens's Huck Finn in influencing early
20th century authors. 2 June 2001.
===========================
Journal article found at site: www.AmerStudies.ubm.edu/
twain/crit/Porter.html: Fred Porter's "Twain's Popularist
Prose and Anti-Popularist Politics." <u>American Studies</u>,
vol 15, #4. December 1997. Essay, 22 pages. Illustra-
tions. accessed: May 12, 2001
===========================
Les B. Readun, Subject Line: Keeping Twain in Perspective; received from discussion group,
AmLitDisGroup@USCC.edu   ;posted/read 16 May 2001.
===========================
<u>American Studies</u> Journal article, www.AmerStudies.ubm.
edu/twain/biblio/Helim.html: Leo Helim,"A Select Twain
[S. L. Clemens] Bibliography." vol 14, #2 June 1996.
13pp; download date: 02JUN98.
===========================
Sarah Lawrence, "Willa Cather's Sense of Frontier."
Article at telnet site, UVLV.edu/amlit20c/criticism/
lawrence_cather.doc
written 17 October 1995 Accessed 4 June 2001
===========================
Sarah Lawrence, email received 14 July 2001; subject: Re:
Cather inquiry.
===========================
Tod Danser, posted 27 April 2001 to alt.fiction.us.dis-
cussion; the Fiction Forum; subject: From the Clemens
vital records in Hannibal MO. downloaded June 17, 2001.

MLA DOCU 4, MLA Manuscript Format

A page of a student paper that should follow MLA guidelines appears on the next page. Lettered line segments mark a number of elements on the page. Complete the following list by indicating next to each letter the appropriate margin, position, or spacing. The first one is done for you as an example.

In addition, there are nine formatting flaws in this sample page; list them and describe what should have been done instead. Use the spaces provided.

      (a) <u>top of page</u> to <u>last name/page number</u>: 1/2 inch

1.   **(b)** top and bottom margins:

2.   **(c)** linespacing:

3.   **(d)** left margin:

4.   **(e)** right margin:

5. _____

6. _____

7. _____

8. _____

9. _____

10. _____

11. _____

12. _____

13. _____

(b)

(c)

(a)

Lorem ipsum dolor sit amet, consectetuer adipiscing elit, sed diam nonummy nibh euismod tincidunt ut laoreet dolore magna aliquam erat volutpat.

MAJOR HEADING

Duis autem vel eum iriure dolor in hendrerit in vulputate velit esse molestie consequat, abitando quest'anno in toscano. Vel illum dolore eu feugiat nulla facilisis at vero eros et accumsan -- iusto odio dignissim qui blandit.

(e)

(d)

Subheading

Ut wisi enim ad minim veniam, quis nostrud exerci tation ullamcorper suscipit lobortis nisl ut aliquip ex ea commodo consequat. Duis autem vel eum iriure dolor in hendrerit in vulputate velit esse molestie;consequat, vel illum dolore eu feugiat nulla facilisis at vero eros et accumsan et iusto odio dignissim qui blandit praesent luptatum:

> "Delenit augue duis dolore te feugait nulla facilisi. Lorem ipsum dolor sit amet, consectetuer adipiscing elit, sed...nonummy aliquam erat volutpat. Ut wisi enim ad minim veniam, quis nostrud aliquip ex ea commodo consequat."

Duis autem vel eum iriure dolor in hendrerit in vulputate velit esse molestie consequat, vel illum dolore eu

(b)

MLA DOCU 4, reference page (with errors)

Chapter 15

OTHER SYSTEMS
OF DOCUMENTATION

OTHER DOCU 1b, APA-Style References

This two-part exercise is based on the research process of a student preparing a paper that must follow APA conventions. You are supplied with a computer printout compiled by the student using an electronic card catalog. Using this printout you are asked to do two things:

(1) prepare bibliography cards; (Use the blank note cards provided.)
(2) compile these cards into a "References" section that incorporates all these cards into a *single* list. (Use a separate sheet of paper.)

Note that the computer printout *does not use* the APA conventions that you need to follow.

For example, given the following printout:

```
Jammesin, Stewart.
Consciousness in America: One Hundred Years of Adver-
tising and Consumerism.
286 p. : illus, biblio
Rutland, Vermont, Conners Press. 1994
GH3448 .J420  1994
```

You would create this APA-style bibliography card:

Jammesin, S. (1994). *Consciousness in America:*

One hundred years of advertising and con-

sumerism. Rutland, VT: Conners Press.

GH3448
.J420
1994

And you would create this entry in your paper's References section:

Jammesin, S. (1994). *Consciousness in America: One hundred years of*

advertising and consumerism. Rutland, VT: Conners Press.

Card Catalog Printout:

Josephson, Matthew.
A Short History of the Blues. 184 p.
New York, NY: Melody House, 1967.
MN254   .J691 1967

Garraty, Jon B., editor.
The Musical '50's. 324 p. : illus.
Chicago: University of Chicago Press, 1982.
MN248   .G12 1982

Takaki, Philip.
A Musical History of the United States. 686 p. : Illus. Biblio.
New York, NY: Meridiun Press, 1993.
MM222   .T449 1993

Jameson, MaryBeth.
"A Blue Note Discography " in William Cantor and Bruce Derries,
eds., pp 114-161, in A Fine Blue Note.
Boston, MA: Thwickham & Burley, 1988.
MN438   .J21 1988

Baxandall, Richard, Linda Gordono, and Susan Rooli, editors.
Hard Singing, Hard Living: American Women Who Sang the Blues.
New York, NY: Phantom Press, 1983.
MM438   .B376 1983

Schlesinger, Peter J. Jr., ed.
In Their Own Voices: An Oral History of 20th Century American
Jazz. 433 p. : Illus. CD-ROM included.
Kansas City, KS: JazzHouse, 1995
MN437   .S993 1995

Guenter, Larry.
Up All Night: A History of the Blues. 420 p. : Biblio.
New York, NY: Melody Press, 1990
MN437   .G554 1990

Gutman, Stanley N.
The Music Business. 384 p. : illus. , biblio.
New York, NY: Phantom Press, 1977.
MN439   .G229 1977

McLaughlin, Gloria. "Uptown, Downtown: Jazz and Socioeconomic
Status"
The Journal of Musical History, 2. April 1971. 299-314.

American Jazz Museum.
All That Jazz!: America's Truest Voice. 448 p. : biblio.
Phoenix, AZ: Fine Press, 1975
MN437   .A99 1975

OTHER DOCU 1c, APA Manuscript Format

A page of a student paper that should follow APA guidelines appears on the next page. Lettered line segments mark a number of elements on the page. Complete the following list by indicating next to each letter the appropriate margin, position, or spacing. The first one is done for you as an example.

In addition, there are nine formatting flaws in this sample page; list them and describe what should have been done instead. Use the spaces provided.

    (a) <u>top of page</u> to <u>last name/page number</u>: 1/2 inch

1. **(b)** top and bottom margins:

2. **(c)** linespacing:

3. **(d)** left margin:

4. **(e)** right margin:

5. _____

6. _____

7. _____

8. _____

9. _____

10. _____

11. _____

12. _____

13. _____

(b)

(a)

(c)

Lorem ipsum dolor sit amet, consectetuer adipiscing elit, sed diam nonummy. Nibh euismod tincidunt ut laoreet dolore magna aliquam erat volutpat.

MAJOR HEADING

Duis autem vel eum iriure dolor in hendrerit in vulputate velit esse molestie consequat, abitando quest'anno in toscano. Vel illum dolore eu feugiat nulla facilisis at vero eros et accumsan et iusto odio dignissim qui blandit.

(e)

(d) **Subheading**

Ut wisi enim ad minim veniam, quis nostrud exerci tation ullamcorper suscipit lobortis nisl ut aliquip ex ea commodo consequat. Duis autem vel eum iriure dolor in hendrerit in vulputate velit esse molestie consequat, vel illum dolore eu feugiat nulla facilisis at vero eros et accumsan et iusto odio dignissim qui blandit praesent luptatum:

> "Delenit augue duis dolore te feugait nulla facilisi. Lorem ipsum dolor sit amet, consectetuer adipiscing elit, sed diam nonummy aliquam erat volutpat. Ut wisi enim ad minim veniam, quis nostrud aliquip ex ea commodo consequat."

Duis autem vel eum iriure dolor in hendrerit in vulputate velit esse molestie consequat, vel illum dolore. Vel illum dolore eu feugiat nulla facilisis at vero eros et accumsan et iusto odio dignissim qui blandit.

(b)

OTHER DOCU 1c, reference page (with errors)

SELECTED

ANSWERS

TO

EXERCISES

COMPOSING

COMP 5c, Proofreading

See your instructor.

PARAGRAPHS

PARA 1, Unity

1. <u>Mental models, our conceptual models of the ways objects work, events take place, or people behave, result from our tendency to form explanations of things</u>. These models are essential in helping us understand our experiences, predict the outcomes of our actions, and handle unexpected occurrences. ~~Unexpected occurrences can happen at any time~~. We base our models on whatever knowledge we have, real or imaginary, naive or sophisticated.

   [Source: modified from Norman, Donald A. *The Psychology of Everyday Things*. NY: Basic, 1988. 38.]

2. <u>The market is as much a part of your company as you are.</u> After all, it represents one-half of the ledger. To grow, your business must earn the permission of the marketplace. No concept is more important for the start-up entrepreneur. ~~Guarantees are an essential component.~~ The customer must give your business permission to sell to him. He does this (at least as a repeat customer) only after a thorough assessment of you, your product or service, and your operation. This is why Detroit is having trouble selling cars even though they're better built than they were. ~~Fortunately this hasn't been a problem in the U.S. aerospace industry.~~ These cars have to overcome years of bad notices. It will take time to accomplish this. In fact, it may take until there's a complete turnover in the market—until those of us who now think Japanese or German no longer drive.

   [Source: modified from Hawken, Paul. *Growing a Business*. NY: Simon & Schuster, 1987. 175-176.]

3. <u>A classical understanding sees the world primarily as underlying form it-self. A romantic understanding sees it primarily in terms of immediate appearance.</u> If you were to show an engine or a mechanical drawing or an electronic schematic to a romantic it is unlikely he would see much in it. It has no appeal because the reality he sees is its surface. Dull, complex lists of names, lines and numbers. Nothing interesting. ~~Classification systems may say more about their creators than about the objects being classi-fied.~~ But if you were to show the same blueprint or schematic or give the same description to a classical person, he might look at it and then be-come fascinated by it because he sees that within the lines and shapes and symbols is a tremendous richness of underlying form.

[Source: modified from Pirsig, Robert M. *Zen and the Art of Motorcycle Maintenance.* NY: Bantam, 1974. 66.]

4. <u>At a certain season of our life we are accustomed to consider every spot as the possible site of a house.</u> I have thus surveyed the country on every side within a dozen miles of where I live. In imagination I have bought all the farms in succession, for all were to be bought, and I knew their price. ~~I enjoy walking and find it a healthful relaxation.~~ I walked over each farmer's pre-mises, tasted his wild apples, discoursed on husbandry with him, and took his farm at his price.

[Source: modified from Thoreau, H. D. *Walden.* Princeton: PUP, 1971. 81.]

5. As the rules of chess define the game of chess, <u>linguistic rules define the game of language, which would not exist without them.</u> They are not strict mechanism of cause and effect—one thing simply making another thing happen—but a system essentially open and incomplete, so that it is al-ways capable of novelty. Rules of etiquette close off a system, keeping it uniform and predictable unless the rules are changed. ~~Who is allowed to changes these rules? When can such changes be made?~~ Rules of language are indirect and can be used again and again on the same finite set of let-ters and words, making possible an open universe of new sentences on the closed universe of the dictionary. ~~Dictionaries you will have noticed are printed, not spoken.~~

[Source: modified from Campbell, Jeremy. *Grammatical Man.* NY: Simon & Schuster, 1982. 127.]

PARA 2b, Development Strategies 1

1. Donald Norman's *The Psychology of Everyday Things*:
   definition; cause and effect
2. Paul Hawken's *Growing a Business*:
   definition; examples
3. Robert Pirsig's *Zen and the Art of Motorcycle Maintenance*:
   classification; contrast
4. Henry David Thoreau's *Walden*:
   narration
5. Jeremy Campbell's *Grammatical Man*:
   analogy; comparison; examples

PARA 2b, Development Strategies 2

Many different strategies could be used, depending on the information you gather, your approach to the material, and your audience. Here are some possibilities:

1. definition; comparison and contrast; facts and statistics
2. definition; comparison and contrast
3. facts and statistics (to quantify recycling); cause and effect (to discuss the rate of adoption)
4. definition, likely including facts and statistics; cause and effect
5. comparison and contrast; narration

PARA 3, Coherence 1

See your instructor.

PARA 3, Coherence 2

See your instructor.

PARA 3, Coherence 3

See your instructor.

GRAMMAR ESSENTIALS

GRAM 1a, Verbs

1. Tina <u>swims</u> in the pool on Tuesdays.
    Vi
2. John <u>gave</u> <u>Fred</u> <u>a birthday present</u>.
    Vt   IO   DO
3. The weather <u>seems</u> <u>fine</u> today.
                VI   PA
4. Shelby <u>bought</u> <u>her textbooks</u> at the campus bookstore.
            Vt   DO
5. Jorge <u>is</u> <u>a tenor</u>.
        VI   PN

GRAM 1b, Nouns

	singular	plural	sing. possessive	pl. possessive
1.	dish	dishes	dish's	dishes'
2.	hero	heroes	hero's	heroes'
3.	book	books	book's	books'
4.	wife	wives	wife's	wives'
5.	man	men	man's	men's

GRAM 1c, Pronouns

1. <u>I</u> gave Donald a call.
2. <u>I</u> spoke to <u>him</u> yesterday.
3. <u>He</u> usually has to call <u>me</u> back.
4. Raspberries are ready at <u>their</u> farm.
5. <u>Which</u> farm, McGuire's?

GRAM 1d, Adjectives

1. If presented with Häagen-Dazs and Ben & Jerry's, could you say which is
   (creamy, <u>creamier</u>, creamiest)?

2. The <u>Washington Post</u> declined to name the (good, better, <u>best</u>) candidate amongst the five potential nominees.

3. Jack is (old, <u>older</u>, oldest) than his brother John.

4. Jack is the (old, older, <u>oldest</u>) of the four children.

5. Before starting the 108 riders, the judge called, "May the (good, better, <u>best</u>) cyclist win!"

GRAM 1e, Adverbs

1. John runs <u>fast</u>.

2. Of all the sopranos, Lena sang the <u>most beautifully</u>.

3. The commute home <u>always</u> seemed longer than the one to the office.

4. After the thunderstorm, steam rose <u>eerily</u> from the <u>still</u> warm pavement.

5. Jackson was tired but worked <u>hard</u> to finish the assigned reading before going to bed.

GRAM 1f, Prepositions

1. (<u>On</u> the move) (<u>since</u> dawn), the hikers had advanced twenty miles (<u>by</u> lunchtime).

2. Sara finished three (<u>of</u> the four essay questions) quickly.

3. Chu's nieces and nephews danced (<u>around</u> the room).

4. Bill saw his token roll (<u>into</u> the street) and disappear (<u>down</u> a storm drain).

5. Forty-seven stories (<u>above</u> the street), the falcons built their nest (<u>on</u> one (<u>of</u> the Chrysler Building's gargoyles)).

GRAM 1g, Conjunctions

1. I went to the store (<u>before</u> Sushmito arrived). (SUB)

2. It rained all night, (<u>so</u> the tournament was postponed). (COORD)

3. I like to fish even (<u>though</u> I don't catch anything most days). (SUB)

4. (<u>Although</u> Melville's <u>Moby Dick</u> is a great book), there are some chapters that are slow reading. (SUB)

5. Professor Pham asked us (<u>not only</u> to compare and contrast Melville and Thoreau, <u>but also</u> to use one or more of their works to support our points). (CORREL)

GRAM 2a, Subjects

1. <u>My dog</u> sleeps so much that my roommate thinks she's a stuffed animal.
2. <u>Ly's enthusiasm for our annual reunion</u> is infectious.
3. <u>Joan's track and swimming talents</u> earned her a scholarship.
4. <u>Calculus 201 and Chemistry 137</u> have kept me extremely busy this semester.
5. <u>The university</u> has five libraries.

GRAM 2b, Predicates

1. Smoking <u>is expensive and addictive.</u>
2. Juan <u>believed that his studies were a worthwhile investment.</u>
3. Melissa's research paper <u>explored the differences between personal debt and the national debt.</u>
4. Gwen <u>is the oldest of five children.</u>
5. Bill and Ted <u>cooked dinner together most nights.</u>

GRAM 3b, Verbals

1. I love <u>running</u> because it requires so little equipment. (GER)
2. <u>Pacing yourself</u> during an exam is crucial. (GER)
3. The drummer <u>playing the timbales</u> is my cousin. (PRES PART)
4. The Continental Army, <u>faced with many hardships</u>, managed <u>to defeat</u> the <u>better trained and equipped British</u>. (PAST PART; INF; PAST PART)
5. <u>To conduct good science</u> requires first good <u>training</u>; second, good insight; and third, great effort. (INF; GER)

GRAM 4, Clauses

1. <u>When I saw Roger</u>, <u>who was just returning from a trip</u>, he told me <u>he would be playing softball with us this Saturday</u>. (ADV CLS; ADJ CLS; NOUN CLS)
2. Ceilia painted her house purple <u>because it was her favorite color</u>. (ADV CLS)
3. <u>If you hit or tip a ball foul and you already have two strikes</u>, the count remains unchanged. (ADV CLS)

4. He hoped <u>his contribution to the charity would benefit [whoever was most in need]</u>. (NOUN CLS [NOUN CLS])

5. After losing three games straight, the team was ebullient <u>when it beat the undefeated first place team</u>. (ADV CLS)

GRAM 5, Types of Sentences

1. Though ordinary ink may look black, it also contains red pigment. (complex)

2. Fred likes to read in bed. (simple)

3. <u>The Grapes of Wrath</u> and <u>Of Mice and Men</u> are examples of books more acclaimed popularly than critically. (simple)

4. After scooping ice cream all summer, my right arm was so strong that I could beat my older brother in arm wrestling, and my left arm looked so withered to me that it seemed almost vestigial, like the forelegs of <u>Tyrannosaurus rex</u>. (compound-complex)

5. Though it may sound odd, I swim in the winter and ski in the summer. (complex)

ESL BASICS

AN IMPORTANT REMINDER FOR STUDENTS: As noted in the exercise book's Preface, because of the flexibility of the English language there may be more than one way to correct the errors in each exercise; this is particularly true in this chapter. If you have any questions about your answers versus the ones supplied in the Selected Answers section, please ask your instructor. Very likely there will be other students with the same or similar questions.

ESL 1a, Modals

1. In or e hour I will be done.
2. You will see me there tonight.
3. I should be able to finish this novel before class. —or—
   I can finish this novel before class.
4. We cannot come to the party.
5. When I was growing up, my family would usually take a trip in the summer.

ESL 1b, Perfect Tenses

1. They have traveled too much this year to want to go on another trip soon.
2. We had expected you yesterday.
3. Bill goes to the movies frequently; he will have seen that one already.
4. Chloë had sung in the choir for three years before she was chosen to be its director.
5. Suzanne has brought me flowers every year on my birthday.

ESL 1c, Progressive Tenses

1. John is seeing Reno for the first time.
2. Sheila is giving her friends dancing lessons.
3. The ozone layer has been thinning because of the release of CFCs.
4. Han is happy today.
5. Sanga had been thinking calculus was easy until he took the midterm exam.

ESL 1d, Passive Voice 1

1. The NHL championship was won by Montreal this year.
2. Africa is visited by many Americans.
3. We were seated by the hostess.
4. Many books are now published only in paperback.
5. Every student is expected to do well in his or her studies.

ESL 1d, Passive Voice 2

1. Terusuke lost my backpack yesterday.
2. Every day many commuters see the Marine Works fountain.
3. Bizet wrote _Carmen_.
4. Many people enjoy reading.
5. My parents saved money scrupulously.

ESL 1e, Two-Word Verbs

1. Where's the newspaper? Oh, John threw it away?
2. The teacher called on the student.
3. Because of the extensive fire damage, the Fire Marshal ordered the building's owners to tear it down.
4. Simone heard from her best friend.
5. Why doesn't he pick on someone his own size?

ESL 1f, Verbals

1. They agreed to come over here before the game.
2. Josef misses eating home-cooked meals.
3. The boss permitted me to take time off when my sister was married.
4. I imagine flying is wonderful.
5. When I finish eating, I'll read to you.

ESL 2a–c, Count and Noncount Nouns 1

1. Gordon knows a lot of local history.
2. How many loaves of bread did Orlo ask us to pick up? —or—
   How many types of bread did Orlo ask us to pick up?

3. Howard used two hundred pails of sand to build his huge sand castle.

4. Guadalupe said many machines are built there.

5. Don't put too much salt in the soup!

ESL 2a–c, Count and Noncount Nouns 2

1. Gianni lost his cash through a hole in his pocket.

2. Their new furniture is beautiful.

3. Are there many students in your history class?

4. Is Karen still looking for a place to live?

5. The poet read her pieces with a lot of confidence.

ESL 2c–d, Articles

1. An hour ago he left for the office.

2. The president is the former governor of Texas.

3. When she finishes high school she wants to travel before finding employment.

4. It was a hot day so we went to the beach.

5. She worked for General Electric before joining Intel.

ESL 2d, Definite Article

1. [To the waiter:] May I have some ketchup please?

   [Later, when it's already on the table:] Please pass the ketchup.

2. Mount Katahdin is the highest peak in Maine.

3. I saw the professor who won the Nobel Prize last year.

4. Hockey is very popular here.

5. I saw Bob walking down the hall just a minute ago.

ESL 3a, Cumulative Adjectives

1. a long white pearl necklace

2. my first new bicycle

3. five small square buildings

4. an ancient brick fireplace

5. seven large triangular windows

ESL 3b, Present and Past Participles

1. Lola found the novel's ending surprising.
2. The winter winds here are very drying.
3. Sofia found organic chemistry fascinating.
4. Jackie's remarks annoyed me.
5. The kitchen scene in <u>Jurassic Park</u> was frightening.

ESL 3c, Adverbs

1. The president traditionally addresses the Congress in January.
2. There never seems to be enough time.
3. My older sister is always helpful.
4. I drove fast enough to get to work on time.
5. Ving typically went to the museum with his father.

ESL 4a–c, Prepositions 1

1. I went to the movies nearly every week.
2. Francesca reads the newspaper to improve her English.
3. When we first moved to Toronto, I missed Hong Kong very much.
4. Sari shops in the grocery store everyday.
5. After his Fulbright in Sardinia, New England looked very green to him.

ESL 4d–f, Prepositions 2

1. Frederico was aware of the problem.
2. My brother's new glasses are for reading.
3. I walked as far as Main Street before discovering that I had left my wallet at home.
4. How much is that equal to in dollars?
5. I like to paint as well as to draw.

ESL 5a–b, Omitted Verbs and Subjects

1. My school has three libraries. It will begin construction of a fourth soon.
   —or—

   My school has three libraries and will begin construction of a fourth soon.

2. Dirk's whole family is very amusing.

3. The baseball league begins its season next week.

4. This reading assignment is very long.

5. The cicadas in the trees in my neighborhood sing all day.

ESL 5c, Expletives

1. There are three interstate highways into downtown Atlanta.

2. Here are my top choices for the position.

3. Here is the best recipe I have for turkey stuffing.

4. It is unlikely to rain when the sky is so clear.

5. There are many golf courses in Chittenden County.

ESL 6b, Questions with Who, Whom, and What

1. Who is coming to dinner?

2. What creates congressional gridlock?

3. Whom did the president nominate?

4. Who brings in today's mail?

5. What does the committee do?

ESL 6c, Indirect Questions

1. How will they finance the new day-care center?

2. Which astronomer identified and named M31?

3. Why did my family come to this country in 1848?

4. Where was the smoke coming from?

5. How does the U.S. Congress differ from the British Parliament?

ESL 6c, Indirect Questions

1. He asked if I was coming or not.

2. Rupert wasn't sure when the Battle of Hastings occurred.

3. We tried to see where the rocket went.

4. The committee researched why the cost of education has outpaced inflation in the last ten years.

5. Everice asked whether I enjoy playing racquetball.

ESL 6d, Reported Speech

1. Nino said that he loves zucchini almost as much as he loves peppers.
2. Bob told me, "I am working in the library five nights per week."
3. With a grin, Erin opined that Roger had played a faltering but passionate cello for years.
4. Mary announced, "I will be running in the Bay to the Breakers race this year."
5. The company spokesperson said to wait for the third quarter results.

ESL 6e, Conditional Sentences

1. If he sees a shooting star, he makes a wish.
2. If you practice enough, you can join a band.
3. If I had practiced more, I might have had my own band.
4. Wherever Fleetwood Mac performed last year, they found big audiences.
5. If Al Gore had been elected, what changes would he have made?

SENTENCES

SENT 1, Parallelism
Possible rewrites:

1. We will see Rufus on Tuesday, and Tito on Wednesday.
2. Though he could not swim, he would not wear a life jacket.
3. El Niño has remained active in the Pacific, and the rain has continued to fall.
4. Congress has forgotten both the individual citizen and personal responsibility.
5. As the sun rose, the moon set.

SENT 2, Misplaced and Dangling Modifiers
Possible rewrites:

1. The tools Don returned to Phil were covered with grease.
2. The EPA wrote new rules for the spotted owl, which was threatened with extinction.
3. I saw him on the green walkway.
4. Young and inexperienced, Jim discovered that jobs were few and far between.
5. I wrote directions to the house for my friend.

SENT 3a–c, Shifts 1

1. The United Nations' membership has grown steadily, and it adds one or more new members nearly every year. (number shift)
2. When I study, I usually work for at least three hours. (tense shift)
3. Once people swim in this lake, especially in August, they never want to swim anywhere else. (person shift)
4. My father worked for 42 years; he retired last month. (tense shift)
5. Let's take the 10:37 train to St. Louis. (person and mood shifts)

SENT 3d–g, Shifts 2

1. I went to the new restaurant on Elm Street and enjoyed the meal. (subject shift)

2. Recycling newsprint requires extensive sophisticated processing, such as the de-inking of paper and the handling of the heavy metals extracted. (style shift)

3. Arlene said, "I read an interesting story in the San Francisco Chronicle and you should read it too." (quotation shift)

4. We sat on the broken down bus until the Transit Authority sent a replacement. (subject shift; dangling modifier)

5. The school's main entrance was an imposing series of granite steps and landings leading up to a pair of great carved oak doors. Inside, the hallways were dark and long. (perspective shift: outside view to inside view)

SENT 4, Irrelevant Detail

1. Marx said that religion is the opium of the people.

2. Charles Dickens was a prolific author, working on up to three novels concurrently.

3. Lately the president has proposed elevating several governmental posts to the rank of cabinet officer.

4. Last Thanksgiving Chuck saw the Matisse retrospective.

5. The interstate highway system is now badly in need of extensive rebuilding.

SENT 4b, Mixed or Illogical Constructions

1. He said that the new bridge won't increase anybody's taxes.

2. They chatted like two birds until they tired.

3. The triple chocolate cake, my best dessert, was always delicious.

4. My brother wrote me a letter last week and I read it two or three times over.

5. I don't know anything about Wagner's opera Parsifal.

SENT 5a, Subordination

Possible rewrites:

1. Bill and Metsa, who started dating five years ago in high school, think they will get married next year.

2. Because Allan Iverson is so fast, he plays both offense and defense well.

3. I do my research at our university library because its one million plus volumes provide coverage that is both in-depth and up-to-date.

4. Stirring constantly to ensure that the butter will not brown, heat the sauce over a low flame.

5. The Statue of Liberty, a gift of the French people and dedicated in 1886, was restored for its centennial and once again looks beautiful.

SENT 5c, Coordination

Possible rewrites:

1. I had a lot of reading to do every day; therefore, I did not watch television at all for months.

2. She agrees with many things Roberto tells her, but when she doesn't, she argues with him.

3. My great uncle neither smokes nor drinks.

4. He likes not only classical music but also country and western.

5. This rain is good for people; it is filling the reservoirs.

SENT 6a, Emphasis

Possible rewrites:

1. Phil told me that once the band got going and people began to dance, Hogan's party was a great success.

2. In New England, not heeding a winter storm warning can be a grave mistake.

3. I was thrilled when I first heard the plan, but now I'm not so sure.

4. Pedro is glad he took his new job, because it is challenging.

5. Because <u>Carmen</u> is Luis's favorite opera, he has seen it eight times.

SENT 6b, Logical Order

Possible rewrites:

1. We arrived at the Grand Canyon, loaded our packs, and hiked to the Colorado River a mile below.

2. Boggs had an awful day when we were at Fenway; he struck out in the first, fifth, and seventh innings.

3. I like a movie if it has a good story, is acted well, and ends happily.

4. In the next three hours I need to mow the lawn, shower and shave, and dress to go out.

5. As I looked around the dimly lit attic, I saw dusty boxes, piles of old clothes, and a complete human skeleton.

SENT 6c, Active Voice
Possible rewrites:

1. Paul was bitten by mosquitoes, black flies, and chiggers on his canoe trip down the Allegash.

2. Griffey hit the ball deep to center.

3. The family bought a new puppy.

4. Kurt's birthday was celebrated by everyone in our dorm.

5. Patrick called me as soon as he returned to Seattle.

SENT 7a, Sentence Variety 1
Possible rewrites:

1. Because it rained for a month, there was great flooding.

2. Vermont has a long winter, but now that I ski it seems shorter.

3. After singing every Sunday in church for years, my parents stopped last year, and now they miss it.

4. As you fly over any major U.S. city, look out the plane's window; you will be shocked by the number of swimming pools you will see.

5. Up at 5 a.m. every day, Anne never misses her gymnastics practice.

SENT 7b, Sentence Variety 2
Possible rewrites:

1. To forget all about their cares for the evening, Roland and Lynda walked in the park.

2. Walking in the park for the evening, Roland and Lynda forgot all about their cares.

3. While Roland and Lynda walked in the park for the evening, they forgot all about their cares.

4. But Roland and Lynda, walking in the park for the evening, forgot all their cares.

5. In the park, Roland and Lynda walked and forgot all their cares for the evening.

EDITING FOR GRAMMAR

EDIT 1a–d, Subject–Verb Agreement 1

1. The ticket, including dinner with dessert, a floor show, and dancing after, costs only twenty dollars.

2. The smell of the ripening apples and pears attracts bees to the orchard.

3. Neither my parents nor my brother wants to try my latest culinary triumph: cranberry-tofu meat loaf.

4. The House's minority make their voices heard.

5. High tides and wind create dangerous conditions along the coast.

EDIT 1e–l, Subject–Verb Agreement 2

1. Anyone who studies regularly will do better in school and enjoy it more.

2. All the explanations are inadequate.

3. None of my classes meets before 10 a.m.

4. There are, on a regulation baseball team, nine players.

5. Politics both fascinates and repulses him.

EDIT 2a–b, Principal Parts of Irregular Verbs

1. If you bend the pipe more, I think it will fit.

2. After John sat down, he pulled out a book and dozed off.

3. Having taken the subway for years, I was not easily surprised by unusual-looking passengers.

4. Paul took the dinner roast out at noon because it was frozen.

5. Having dug the trench, the workers laid the new gas line.

EDIT 2c, Verb Tense

1. PRESENT PERFECT: I have gone to the All-Star Game every year.

2. PRESENT PROGRESSIVE: I am going to the All-Star Game this year.

3. PRESENT PERFECT PROGRESSIVE: I have been going to the All-Star Game every year.

4. PAST: I went to the All-Star Game every year until last year.

5. PAST PERFECT: I had gone to the All-Star Game every year until last year.

EDIT 2e, Verb Mood

1. (subjunctive) Bob asked that he come early today.

IMPERATIVE: Come early today.

2. (subjunctive) If I were training harder, I would be better prepared.

INDICATIVE: Because I was training harder, I was better prepared.

3. (indicative) Every night he reads until bedtime.

SUBJUNCTIVE: I asked that he read every night until bedtime.

4. (imperative) Mary said, "Hurry up, or we'll miss the bus."

INDICATIVE: Mary told us to hurry up or we'd miss the bus.

5. (subjunctive) I wished it were snowing, but it was only raining.

INDICATIVE: I wished for snow, but got only rain.

EDIT 2f, Active and Passive Voices

1. (passive) The letters were mailed by Jamal after lunch.

2. (active) Raoul cooked the dinner.

3. (passive) Angle of Repose was written by Wallace Stegner.

4. (passive) The Blue Line bus was seen by Regina.

5. (active) Many people who rarely watch baseball otherwise, watch the World Series.

EDIT 3a, Pronoun Agreement

1. The faculty votes for its officers every October.

2. He needs to better train his dog Biff, who barks at the letter carrier every day.

3. Neither Mrs. Williams nor Mr. Williams remembered her or his birthday.

4. When Louisa and Hal come to visit, they always bring their dog.

5. Each player in the tournament took a turn at the table.

EDIT 3b, Pronoun Reference

1. Last night on the Charlotte-Hinesburg Road, Adriano saw eight deer, which was unusual.

2. Professor Marilee Tecknor, who studies retroviruses and has isolated a new subclass, gave a lecture on retroviruses at our seminar.

3. Though I know that supply-side economics focuses on production, and demand-side economics emphasizes consumption, this knowledge has never helped me understand where my paycheck goes every week.

4. When the company demanded a cut in wages and benefits, the union leadership recommended a strike vote be taken.

5. When tours come through our town, they often stop at the Shelburne Museum to see its extensive American folk art collection.

EDIT 3c, Pronoun Case 1

1. Have you seen my brother?
2. After taking the A train, Chuck and I went to the deli.
3. If it were up to Laura and me, we'd leave now.
4. The boss appreciated their working on Saturday night.
5. My sister said she would be going to visit our grandmother after visiting Susan and me.

EDIT 3c–d, Pronoun Case 2

1. Professor Mbutuze asked Dave and me to participate in the experiment.
2. Despite all his campaigning, the New York Times reported that the incumbent was running stronger than he.
3. My sister, who has incredibly acute hearing when it comes to the telephone, yelled out from the shower, "Whom is that call for?"
4. With two runners on, Lana and me, our best hitter came to the plate.
5. The victory will go to whoever crosses the finish line first.

EDIT 4, Adjectives and Adverbs

1. Laura grew more and more confident as the semester progressed.
2. I think it's colder today than yesterday.
3. The NRC is charged with monitoring these kinds of nuclear safety issues.

4. He is doing well in pottery class.

5. With two of their starters on the disabled list, things look bad for the Seattle Mariners.

EDIT 5, Sentence Fragments

Possible rewrites:

1. My little brother is 6' 2" and still growing.

2. My big brother Todd swam in high school and dove in college.

3. While on vacation I read two books: Nicholas Evans's <u>The Horse Whisperer</u> and Frances Mayes's <u>Under the Tuscan Sun</u>.

4. Last night I saw Neville and Molly at the student union.

5. When I saw the Mona Lisa in person, I was, to be honest, disappointed.

EDIT 6, Comma Splices

Possible rewrites:

1. Many experts continue to believe that the American Civil War was the earliest instance of modern warfare.

2. Professor Gerson has a pleasantly acid sense of humor; accordingly, he quipped that the term <u>European ally</u> is an oxymoron.

3. I practice conga one hour every day; this has helped me improve a lot in the last year.

4. Spring in San Francisco is cool, and many visitors wish they had brought warmer clothes.

5. I am a business major, so studying economics will give me a useful background.

EDIT 6, Fused Sentences

Possible rewrites:

1. We took a cab to the theatre. We saw <u>Show Boat</u>.

2. I hope Ben will come over and help me adjust my car's carburetor.

3. After it rained for twenty days straight, I felt like escaping to the desert.

4. I know what a typeface is, but I'm not quite sure what a font is.

5. The last U.S. space shuttle flight to Mir was made in 1999; since then, all shuttle flights have been to the new International Space Station.

WORD CHOICE

WORD 1, Eliminating Clutter

Possible answers:

1. Tom is a point guard who can play center when necessary.
2. The test was difficult because it covered the whole semester.
3. Bad weather in Atlanta delayed Bill's two brothers' flight, so we had to wait at the airport for them for five hours.
4. The school band, obviously unpracticed, could not even play the national anthem without mistakes.
5. Why do schools of swimming fish and flocks of flying birds move with a similar coordinated motion?

WORD 2a, Denotation

1. What are the effects of the new spending bill?
   affect: (verb) to change
   effect: (noun) a result; also (verb) to produce
2. Even if you disagree strongly with him, please be civil.
   civic: (adj) relating to a city
   civil: (adj) refraining from rudeness
3. Emile was a voracious reader.
   vociferous: (adj) loud and shouting
   voracious: (adj) eager to devour
4. Sex education has helped many teenagers get factual information on venereal diseases.
   venerable: (adj) worthy of respect
   venereal: (adj) transmitted by sexual intercourse
5. Paul, carried away by the emotional appeal of his own argument, went off on a tangent.
   tangible: (adj) something that can be touched
   tangent (go off on a tangent): (verb) to break from a line of thinking; to digress

WORD 2c, General versus Specific Words
Possible answers:

1. transportation: bus
2. foods: vegetables
3. vegetables: carrots
4. seasons: fall
5. holidays: New Year's

WORD 2c, Abstract versus Concrete Words

1. pretty: abstract
2. justice: abstract
3. leaves: concrete
4. blue: abstract
5. stars: concrete
6. wood: concrete
7. fast: abstract
8. cake: concrete
9. truth: abstract
10. shoes: concrete

WORD 2d, Idioms

1. The committee agreed to the plan.
2. Frieda left early so that she would be sure to get a good seat.
3. My niece insisted that Jell-O was superior to pudding.
4. Though we arrived early, we still had to wait in line.
5. The coach gave me some extra tips to help me try to improve my shot.

WORD 3a, Appropriate Formality
Possible answers:

1. Reggie disliked their new album intensely.
2. Bryan cannot come today.
3. The show was spectacular.
4. Collecting stamps was Phil's hobby.
5. If I have time, I'll eat lunch with you at noon.

WORD 4, Bias in Writing

Possible answers:

1. Our ancestors showed great courage to leave their homelands and voyage to a new and often little-known country.
2. The president was swamped with questions from the reporters.
3. The writing course was tailored to first-year students.
4. Who chairs that Senate subcommittee?
5. Of all creatures on the planet, people are the most intelligent and the most destructive.

WORD 5, The Dictionary

1. There are four syllables in "ob·liv·i·ous," and there are three in "ob·nox·ious."
2. marathon: a race of 26 miles, 385 yards; based upon the length of the run made by a single runner from the Greek city Marathon to Athens to tell of the Greek victory (490 B.C.) over the Persians.
3. lens: from the Latin lentil for the resemblance of a lens to the shape of the lentil bean. The double-convex lens.
4. frankfurter: a sausage originating in Frankfurt, Germany.
5. There are three syllables in "scru·pu·lous."

WORD 6, The Thesaurus

1. **beautiful** (adj): admirable; alluring; attractive; appealing; splendid
   (antonym): ugly
2. **show** (noun): drama; performance; demonstration; exposition; fair
   (verb): bare; reveal; exhibit; expose; divulge
   (antonym): (verb) hide
3. **prise** (verb): lever open; pry open; force; wrench; obtain with difficulty
   (antonym): close
4. **document** (noun): certificate; charter; deed; form; instrument
   (verb): chronicle; list; log; note; write down
   (antonym): (verb) destroy records
5. **industrious** (adj): busy; conscientious; assiduous; diligent; earnest
   (antonym): lazy

WORD 7, Usage

1. I thought we could leave, but Joe is not ready to go.

2. Nicholas loved music of all types, but Lou was very particular.

3. Although I set out 20 tomato plants this summer, none has any ripe fruit yet.

4. The show that is on Channel 42 at 10 tonight should be very interesting.

5. Jason should have arrived by now.

PUNCTUATION

PUNCT 1a–c, The Comma 1

1. He worked hard, yet he was not feeling tired.
2. As Felix watched, the cat ate her breakfast of Tuna Delight.
3. Last semester I had Professor Roop for history, which has always been my favorite subject.
4. Yawning, Mumia put down his book and went to bed.
5. My oldest brother, Geoffrey, usually comes for Thanksgiving.

PUNCT 1d–g, The Comma 2

1. The recipe specifically called for ripe large red tomatoes.
2. This fall Eliot was reading Thomas McGuane, Rick Bass, and Alice Walker.
3. For this reason, the committee voted to change the policy.
4. President Jimmy Carter may turn out to be more effective out of office than in, unlike Lyndon Johnson.
5. Riding into a headwind can help you improve your cycling endurance, power, and technique.

PUNCT 1h–l, The Comma 3

1. I smiled and said, "Yes, I'll be there."
2. If you want to call, Jessye has a phone.
3. Our reservations are for Friday, October 26, through Sunday, November 11.
4. Luke called yesterday and said, "Congratulations on your new baby."
5. Lonnie gave me a ride from Tulsa, Oklahoma, to Paris, Texas.

PUNCT 1m, The Comma 4

1. Adela and her brother watched <u>West Wing</u> every week.
2. I drove last week to Pullman, Washington, to visit my best friends.

3. The critics panned the play <u>Welcome Home</u> as slow and pretentious.

4. If I were you, I would leave before rush hour.

5. The small gold locket was a family heirloom.

PUNCT 2, The Semicolon

1. The drive from Akron to Cincinnati was long, but I didn't mind, nor did my sister.

2. The rapid decrease in computer hardware prices has put pressure on software developers to do the same; nonetheless, they have resisted the trend for the most part.

3. Cn one recent weekend I saw <u>Pearl Harbor</u>, which used extensive computer-generated simulations of an historical event; <u>The Matrix</u>, which explored virtual worlds accessed via mind control; and <u>Until the End of the World</u>, which presented computer-driven dream exploration—technology is both a major theme and tool of the film studios.

4. I was shocked when I drove the new $20,000 car; it rode only a bit better than my current car, which has a book value of only $1,500.

5. Although I support universal access to health care, I disagree with coupling it to flat rating; providing access shouldn't eliminate underwriting entirely.

PUNCT 3, The Colon

1. I have passed along to my children one of my father's sayings: "When you borrow something, try to return it in better condition than you received it."

2. Scientists, in an effort to isolate what it is in food that makes most people evaluate it as "tasting good or delicious," have determined the single most important ingredient: fat.

3. Cn your way home please pick up a pound of cold cuts, a head of lettuce, and a video.

4. Today is a very good day for haying: plenty of sunshine, a light breeze, and low humidity.

5. We took the following route: Route 80 to Rock Springs, Route 187 to Farson, and Route 28 to South Pass City.

PUNCT 4, The Apostrophe

1. Did you see the film My Mother's Castle?

2. My grandmother told me that the '38 hurricane was much worse than this year's storm.

3. A srake sheds its skin when it's growing.

4. What is our company's policy regarding maternity leave?

5. I thought it was hers, but perhaps it's really Bill's.

PUNCT 5, Quotation Marks

1. "Where you place your commas is one of my teacher's 'things,' so I always double check my work," said Elaine.

2. "Would you like to come to dinner with us?" Mary asked.

3. When I read computer magazines I find all the technobabble confusing: RAM, ROM, and bytes—who dreams up these terms?

4. Milan told me that Faulkner wrote the novel As I Lay Dying in only six weeks.

5.   "I hope you'll come to our party tonight," said Alison.

   "Me too," I replied, "but I have to work until 11."

   "That's no problem," she said. "It doesn't even start until 10, and I doubt you'll miss anything. Just come as you are after work."

PUNCT 6a, The Period

1. If you know the Latin meaning abbreviated by a.m. and p.m., you will find it easier to remember which one to use.

2. One of the experimental drugs being used to combat AIDS is AZT.

3. I wondered if he knew what the USDA stamp on the meat stood for.

4. One of the most woeful scenes in all of Shakespeare is in King Lear V.iii.

5. Tintin's best friend is Capt. Horatio Haddock.

PUNCT 6b–c, The Question Mark and Exclamation Point

1. Joyce said, "Do you know whether bus or subway is the better way to get to Avenue J from here?"

2. As usual for this region, the weather was sunny.

3. Which route to Des Moines has less traffic, John wanted to know.

4. "Can I come too?" my sister asked.

5. Louis asked me which class I liked best.

PUNCT 6d–h, Other Punctuation
Possible Rewrites:

1. One awkward, but acceptable, solution to the problem of sexism in pronouns is the use of <u>him/her</u> as well as <u>he or she</u>.

2. When in Rome—as the saying goes—do as the Romans do.

3. The senator said, "The president's position [on Senate Resolution 553] is encouraging and will help him pass his own agenda later in the session."

4. "Our class meets in that new science building. What's its name? Something Hall ... Burstein ... Gurstein? I can't remember," said John.

5. I still remember the opening lines to Shakespeare's Sonnet LXXIII: "That time of year thou mayst in me behold / When yellow leaves, or none, or few, do hang / Upon those boughs which shake against the cold."

MECHANICS

MECH 1a–d, Capitals 1

1. Unfortunately, stargazers living this far north can't see the Southern Cross.
2. When James "Joe" Jackson sang last week at the 3rd Avenue Grill, the crowd roared its approval.
3. The cold war may be over, but we're still paying the bill.
4. The Baptist church in my town sponsors a community food shelf.
5. In the last four months the Missouri and Mississippi rivers reached record flood levels, but the Hudson River was below normal.

MECH 1e–j, Capitals 2

1. In a recent article, commentator Julia Webb wrote, "For the first time in U.S. history, by the year 2002, more than fifty percent of all American jobs will require at least one year of college."
2. I read the <u>Daily Plains Record</u> every day to keep up on local news.
3. During the spring semester Dmitri is going to enroll in calculus, history, and English.
4. I think she bought one of the new Apple notebook computers.
5. Who reports on the news media? The news media do.

MECH 2, Abbreviations

1. He reported to Sergeant Bilko.
2. The president announced that the new policy was designed to protect our national security.
3. Aristotle was born in 384 B.C.
4. Dr. C. Everett Koop gave the keynote address. —or—
   C. Everett Koop, M.D. gave the keynote address. [MD and M.D. are both acceptable]
5. For the trip they packed clothes, food, games, and so forth.

MECH 3, Numbers

1. Armand cut the plank into 4 six-foot sections. [or four 6-foot sections]

2. Charles Lindbergh began his historic two-day flight on May 20, 1927 from Roosevelt Field, Long Island.

3. Skosh thought the boat out to Catalina Island was more than $20. [or twenty dollars]

4. American Airlines currently has over 620 planes.

5. Over the holidays we saw four films, two plays, and thirteen videos. [or 4 films, 2 plays, and 13 videos]

MECH 4, Italics/Underlining

1. Linda likes Microsoft _Word_, but I prefer Claris _MacWrite_.

2. The most commonly occurring word in English is _the_.

3. I asked him to explain what _noblesse oblige_ means.

4. Did you read last week's cover story in _Newsweek_?

5. Tina objected to Dickens's overfrequent use of a _deus ex machina_ to resolve his fantastically-plotted novels.

MECH 5, The Hyphen

1. I am very close to my brother-in-law.

2. The ex-Metropolitan Opera soprano joined our community chorus and improved the entire section's performance.

3. Are you looking forward to the beginning of the school year?

4. Our class voted twenty-one to seventeen for more study time.

5. In pre-revolutionary America the colonists were subjects of the king of England.

MECH 6a, Basic Spelling Rules

1. I'm hoping we can see Jeri before she leaves.

2. Professor Guimard is very knowledgeable about plate tectonics.

3. Lofti Zadeh was lying down thinking when an idea suddenly occurred to him; half an hour later he had laid out all the fundamentals of the field now known as Fuzzy Logic.

4. How much did you say you paid for those peaches?

5. I sent the package via Express, so he ought to receive it by noon tomorrow.

MECH 6b, Words that Sound Alike

1. In our library, serial acquisitions is on the 3rd floor.

2. In the 100-meter finals, Sarah was third and I was fourth.

3. My father is site manager for the new Deeter Building construction project.

4. My teacher recommended that we always read the foreword, as it usually defines the scope and approach of the book that follows.

5. All the people I know with personal stationery are of my parents' generation.

DESIGN

DESIGN 2a–c, Basic Computer Formatting

    (a)   <u>top of page</u> to <u>last name/page number</u>: 1/2 inch

1. (b)   top margin: 1 inch

2. (c)   left margin: 1 inch

3. (d)   bottom margin: 1 inch

4. (e)   right margin: 1 inch

5. (f)   linespacing: double-spaced

WRITING AN ARGUMENT / WRITING ABOUT LITERATURE

ARGUE 1b, Facts versus Claims

1. (claim) Euthanasia is a right that every American should have the option of electing.

2. (fact) Some animal rights advocates object to the use of animals for medical research and testing.
   (claim) It is immoral to use animals for medical research and testing.

3. (fact) The use of grades in schools is traditional in American schools.
   (claim) The use of grades stifles creativity in American schools.

4. (fact) Snowboarding became an Olympic medal sport in 1998.
   (claim) The designation of snowboarding in 1998 as an Olympic sport will serve to promote this sport's development.

5. (fact) U.S. immigration policy still reflects cold war biases.
   (claim) To the detriment of our nation, U.S. immigration policy still reflects cold war biases.

ARGUE 2a, Syllogisms

1. FALLACIOUS. The major premise is false; men other than schoolteachers routinely have chalk on their hands, such as carpenters, tailors, and artists

2. FALLACIOUS. The conclusion is false; although the major and minor premises are true, non-nutritional effects (such as genetics-based diseases) can cause poor health.

3. FALLACIOUS. The conclusion is false; although the major and minor premises are true, the conclusion is false as it mistakenly attributes causation to an event that is merely coincident.

4. FALLACIOUS. The conclusion is false; although the major and minor premises are true, the conclusion is false because animals other than fish live in water (such as lobster and whales).
5. VALID. The major, minor premises and conclusions are all true.

LIT 2, Conventions for Writing about Literature

See your instructor.

SPECIAL KINDS OF WRITING

SPECIAL 1a, E-mail

1. Subject line is blank; it should instead provide some useful indicator of the message's contents.

2. "Prof." instead of Professor—this is the first of a series of excessively informal choices made by the writer. Note that this is a message from a student to his professor; it should not be overly informal. The same standards generally apply to E-mail at work.

3. "b/c" instead of "because"; again, this style is too informal.

4. " ;)" —emoticons are too informal.

5. "IS I¯ TRUE THAT OUR FIRST DRAFT IS DUE MONDAY?" Don't write in all caps; it's like yelling at someone and particularly inappropriate in this context.

SPECIAL 2a, Formatting a Business Letter

(a) top of page to top of return address: 6-12 linespaces (use this variation to balance the letter visually on the page from top to bottom)

1. (b) linespacing: single-spaced throughout
   Check spaces between blocks as they should not all be the same; that is, add space between the date and internal address; internal address and salutation; between the saluation and body text; between text blocks; between the last text block and the close; between the close and signature; and between the signature and notations (if any).

2. (c) left margin; 1 inch

3. (d) bottom margin: in a single-page business letter, such as this one, there is no standard bottom margin; instead the bottom margin floats in accord with how you set the top margin.

4. (e) right margin: 1 inch

5. Appropriate letter type: (full block; modified block; indented)? Full block; it is the most formal and therefore most appropriate for this purpose.

THE RESEARCH PAPER

RESCH 1, Conducting Library and Internet Research

Down

2. Number used to locate books within the stacks. **CALL NUMBER**
3. Acronym for Compact Disc, Read-Only Memory. **CD-ROM**
4. Good source of geographical information, especially maps. **ATLAS**
5. Internet discussion group implemented as subscription-only e-mail. **LISTSERV**
7. General term for magazines, journals, and newspapers. **PERIODICALS**

Across

1. Generally an excellent first resource for a topic new to you. **ENCYCLOPEDIA**
6. Acronym for an Internet site's address. **URL**
9. Source of brief biographical sketches on contemporary Americans. **WHOS WHO IN AMERICA**
12. Author of a very useful guide to the reference books. **SHEEHY**
14. Best-known guide to popular periodical literature. **READERS GUIDE**

RESCH 5b, Avoiding Plagiarism

Because there are infinitely many possible "correct" paraphrases of the quotations provided, it is left to the instructor to review and assess each student's work for this exercise.

RESCH 6, Integrating Borrowed Material

Because there are infinitely many possible "correct" ways to incorporate these quotations, it is left to the instructor to review and assess each student's work for this exercise.

MLA DOCUMENTATION AND FORMAT

MLA DOCU 1, MLA In-Text Citations

Note: Possible answers are provided but many other valid
    solutions exist.

1. The fantasy genre has always supported the concept of a separate,
    sometimes superior, animal wisdom: "Human beings say, 'It never rains but
    it pours.' This is not very apt, for it frequently does rain without pouring.
    The rabbits' proverb is better expressed. They say, 'One cloud feels lonely'"
    (Adams, 184; ch. 23).

2. The fantasy genre has always supported the concept of a separate,
    sometimes superior, animal wisdom. In <u>Watership Down</u>, Richard Adams's
    narrator gently chides the reader: "Human beings say, 'It never rains but it
    pours.' This is not very apt, for it frequently does rain without pouring. The
    rabbits' proverb is better expressed. They say, 'One cloud feels lonely'"
    (184; ch. 23).

3. Though they exist in infinite variety, clouds have a simple shared origin: "A
    cloud is a collection of water droplets or ice crystals in the air. It is formed
    when water vapor is cooled and changed into water droplets or ice crys-
    tals" (Heimler and Neal 234).

4. Heimler and Neal point out in <u>Principles</u> that though clouds exist in infinite
    variety, they have a simple shared origin: "A cloud is a collection of water
    droplets or ice crystals in the air. It is formed when water vapor is cooled
    and changed into water droplets or ice crystals" (234).

5. As Symington observed, "NATO's muddled expansion is so fraught with
    competing strategies that it has simultaneously threatened Moscow and
    made overtures to Russia to join the alliance itself" ("Crossroads" 267).

MLA DOCU 2, MLA List of Works Cited—Electronic Sources

Danser, Tod. "From the Clemens vital
records in Hannibal MO." Online
posting. 27 Apr. 2001 The Fiction
Forum. 17 Jun. 2001
<alt.fiction.us.discussion>.

Helim, Leo. "A Select Twain [S. L.
Clemens] Bibliography." American
Studies 14.2 (1996): 13 pp. 2 Jun.
2001 <http://www.AmerStudies.
ubm.edu/twain/biblio/helim.html>.

Lawrence, Sarah. "Mark Twain." Manifest
Destiny and American Frontier
Literature. Oct. 1996. 22 Jun. 2001
<gopher://unebraska.edu/AmerLit
/essays/SLawrence
/manifest_destiny.doc>.

Lawrence, Sarah. "Re: Cather Inquiry."
E-mail to D. Smith. 14 Jul. 2001.

Lawrence, Sarah. "Willa Cather's
Sense of Frontier." Oct. 1995.
4 June 2001 <telnet://UVLV.edu
/amlit20c/criticism
/lawrence_cather.doc>.

MLA DOCU 4, MLA Manuscript Format

    (a)   <u>top of page</u> to <u>last name/page number</u>: 1/2 inch

1. (b)   top and bottom margins: 1 inch

2. (c)   linespacing: double-spaced

3. (d)   left margin: 1 inch

4. (e)   right margin: 1 inch

5. "Smith page 3" should instead be "Smith 3"— "page" shouldn't be written out.

OTHER SYSTEMS
OF DOCUMENTATION

OTHER DOCU 1b, APA-Style References

American Jazz Museum. (1975). <u>All that</u>
<u>jazz!: America's truest voice.</u> Phoenix,
AZ: Fine Press.

MN437
.A99
1975

Baxandall, R., Gordono, L., & Rooll, S.
(Eds.). (1983). <u>Hard singing, hard liv-</u>
<u>ing: American women who sang the</u>
<u>blues.</u> New York: Phantom Press.

MM438
.B376
1983

Garraty, J. B. (Ed.). (1982). <u>The musical</u>
<u>'50's.</u> Chicago: University of Chicago
Press.

MN248
.G12
1982

Guenter. (1990). <u>Up all night: A history of</u>
<u>the blues.</u> New York: Melody Press.

MN437
.G554
1990

Gutman, S. N. (1977). <u>The music business.</u>
New York: Phantom Press.

MN439
.G229

References

American Jazz Museum. (1975). <u>All that jazz!:</u>
<u>America's truest voice.</u> Phoenix, AZ: Fine
Press.

Baxandall, R., Gordono, L., & Rooli, S. (Eds.).
(1983). <u>Hard singing, hard living: American</u>
<u>women who sang the blues.</u> New York: Phantom
Press.

Garraty, J. B. (Ed.). (1982). <u>The musical '50's.</u>
Chicago: University of Chicago Press.

Guenter, L. (1990). <u>Up all night: A history of the</u>
<u>blues.</u> New York: Melody Press.

Gutman, S. N. (1977). <u>The music business.</u> New York:
Phantom Press.

OTHER DOCU 1c, APA Manuscript Format

    (a)   <u>top of page</u> to <u>last name/page number</u>: 1/2 inch

1. (b)   top and bottom margins: 1 inch

2. (c)   linespacing: double-spaced

3. (d)   left margin: 1 inch

4. (e)   right margin: 1 inch

5. "Smith page 3" should instead be "Rise and Fall   3"-- the student's name is not included, nor is the word "page," and the page number should be preceded by a shortened version of the paper's title (here given as "Rise and Fall").